DATE			

RADIO:
THE GREAT YEARS

IT'S LOVELY, DUCKIE. COME AND TRY IT.

**DON'T SPEND YOUR TIME IN CINEMAS
OR WASTE YOUR QUIDS ON BOOKS
BUT BE LIKE ME, AND HAVE A SPREE
WITH A "WIRELESS – SET – DE – LUXE"**

RADIO:
THE GREAT YEARS

Derek Parker

David & Charles
Newton Abbot   London   North Pomfret (VT)   Vancouver

To
All my good friends at Broadcasting
and Bush Houses

ISBN 0 7153 7430 3

©Derek Parker 1977

Set in 10 on 12 Goudy Old Style by Ronset Ltd, Darwen
and printed in Great Britain
by The Alden Press, Oxford
for David & Charles (Publishers) Limited
Brunel House   Newton Abbot   Devon

Published in the United States of America
by David & Charles Inc
North Pomfret   Vermont 05053   USA

Published in Canada
by Douglas David & Charles Limited
1875 Welch Street   North Vancouver   BC

Contents

LISTENIN'!

"Stand by one minute please, we are going to relay -

-- the Nightingale!"

Foreword

I am of the generation that grew up with radio, and my love affair with it has lasted for over forty years. I remember the distress of having to stay on a sunny beach in Cornwall on a summer Sunday afternoon, rather than rushing back in the Austin 7 in time for the Ovaltinies' programme on Radio Luxembourg. I remember bursting into tears when *Happi-drome* ended its current series: being deprived of the company of Mr Lovejoy, Mr Ramsbottom and Enoch was even worse than being in Miss May's class at the infants' school. I remember weeding furiously along the rows of carrots in the allotment on a Thursday evening, so as to be indoors in time for *ITMA*.

Later, I remember very clearly my first experience of classical music: failing to switch off *Music Hall* the moment it finished, I found myself in the middle of the first movement of Mendelssohn's *Italian Symphony*—and was hooked. That was the year in which I made my first broadcast (from Studio 8, Broadcasting House, Bristol; fee, one guinea).

Wireless seemed to me, as a listener, to be absolute enchantment. The isle was full of noises, and I listened to them all. In a very real sense, I was educated by radio—long before the Open University!

Later, when I started trying to use the medium as a broadcaster, I realised what a difficult medium it is to use well. This book is a tribute to those who have used it well—from A. J. Allen to Tommy Handley to Kenneth Horne to Tony Hancock to the Goons. I have remembered with pleasure, too, the great radio dance bands, the plays and the Proms, the nine o'clock news and Alvar Lidell reading it. . . . And I have tried to convey just how fortunate Britain has been in the BBC. Poor Auntie has taken some knocks in the course of her career, from

7

a number of fists made by a variety of people, from the right-wing press, the left-wing press, the Festival of Light and Women's Lib, from Mr Churchill and Harry Pollitt and Major General (Rtd), Cheltenham. I don't say that I haven't, myself, from time to time desperately wanted to knock her hat over her eyes.

But had I thought of it first, I too would have used as a title the phrase Jack de Manio took as the title of his recollections of his life in radio: 'To Auntie, with love'.

D.P.

I The Wonderful Wireless

Broadcasting really began in Great Britain nineteen years after that astonishing day in December 1901 when Gugliemo Marconi received, in St John's, Newfoundland, signals sent across the Atlantic from Poldhu in Cornwall. Five years later, in America, music and speech were heard 'on the air' for the first time. In 1920 the first competent American radio station opened in Pittsburgh. And in the same year, the Marconi Company began broadcasting from Chelmsford in England.

The Chelmsford broadcasts were pretty vestigial, consisting at first of music played by an *ad hoc* Marconi orchestra of amateur musicians: cornet and oboe, one-string fiddle and piano. A Miss W. Sayers made the first solo broadcast: a sturdy soprano, and somewhat badtemperedly referred to the broadcasts as 'these Punch-and-Judy shows' (much as the novelist Evelyn Waugh always used to refer to BBC engineers as 'the electricians').

Nevertheless, those first broadcasts were heard as far afield as Italy, though 'the electricians' used only a single aerial slung between two 450ft posts. And at the end of February, two broadcasts a day were made, each lasting for thirty minutes, and containing news, live music and gramophone records. For the first time, people began to 'listen in' regularly; and for the first time it was dimly recognised that radio might—just might —become important. Lord Northcliffe, the proprietor of the *Daily Mail*, while uncertain of the value or future of broadcasting, saw it as a good means of publicity, and on 15 June 1920, engaged Dame Nellie Melba, then perhaps the most famous singer in the world, for a broadcast *Daily Mail* concert.

Sweeping into the tiny studio, Dame Nellie delivered herself of one of her magical trills (her 'hello to the world', she said),

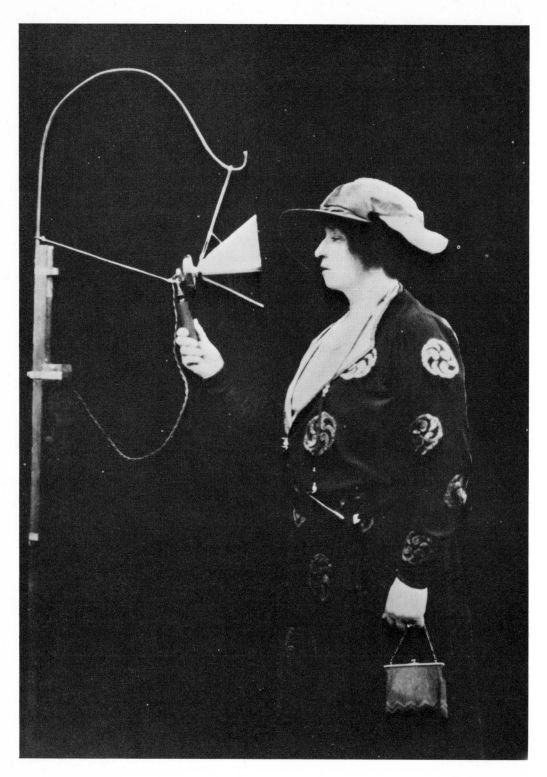

and then gave a short recital. The 'Addio' from *La Bohème* (which she was to broadcast again during her last appearance at Covent Garden in a few years' time) was heard in Newfoundland and Paris, and in the *Daily Mail* offices in London her secretary, who had steadfastly declined to believe in such necromancy as wireless broadcasting, recognised her voice and almost fainted with the realisation that magic was actually being performed.

That single broadcast caught the public imagination; photographs of Melba confronting the microphone appeared all over the world; from 1920 onwards, radio was news. Singers were among the first to embrace the microphone—sometimes too lovingly. Lauritz Melchior, the greatest Wagnerian tenor of his generation, went down to Chelmsford and caused the engineers

Dame Nellie Melba, almost sixty, and with her career as a great opera star nearing its end, sang into the microphone from the Marconi studios at Chelmsford in 1920. This was the first advertised broadcast entertainment
(*The Marconi Company Ltd*)

Lauritz Melchior, one of the finest Wagnerian tenors of his time, broadcast from Chelmsford a few weeks after Melba
(*The Marconi Company Ltd*)

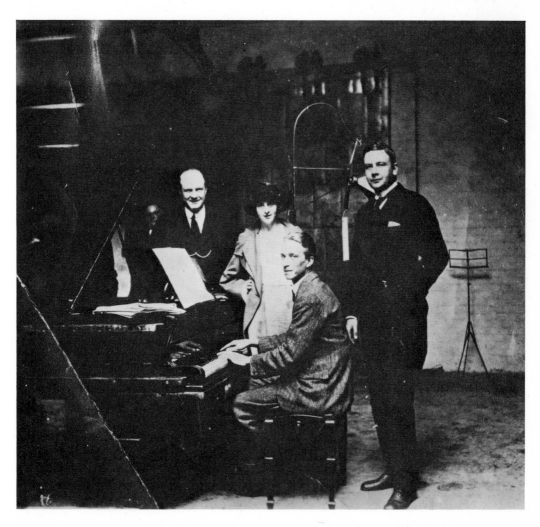

The pianist Myra Hess accompanying Jelly d'Aranyi in a recital broadcast from one of the Savoy Hill studios in December 1928

some trouble by insisting on the theory that the louder he sang the more people would be able to hear him. (He continued to take that view, and when he broadcast from Savoy Hill, the microphone had to be carried into the corridor and the studio door placed ajar, to cope with the volume.)

In 1904, the Wireless Telegraphy Act had made it necessary for all radio transmitters and receivers to be licensed, and the Chelmsford broadcasts were made 'by kind permission of the Post Office'. Though there was some opposition to regular broadcasting, such organisations as The Wireless Society of London (later The Radio Society of Great Britain) pressed for development of the remarkable new means of communication, and, apart from commercial pressure, it was more or less by popular demand that in 1921 the Postmaster General consented to license the Marconi Company to make regular broadcasts from a hut at Writtle, near Chelmsford.

At Writtle gathered several of the men who were later to become prominent members of the staff of the British Broadcasting Company (as it was known at first). Perhaps the most enterprising and imaginative was P. P. Eckersley, an engineer, and head of Marconi's experimental radio section. He intro-duced gramophone records with impromptu comments, encouraged his colleagues to broadcast the first play ever heard on radio—an amateur reading of Edmond Rostand's *Cyrano de Bergerac*—and introduced an 'operatic' programme in which he sang all the parts himself (a precursor of Peter Ustinov's *Mock Mozart*).

Looking back now at that hut at Writtle, one sees a microcosm of the present BBC: drama department, variety department, news and current affairs . . . the single piano to become the many BBC orchestras, the piece of paper with Eckersley's notes, the vast script library. Even the special-effects department was born there: when Writtle went off the air in 1923, a toast was drunk in water, introduced by the sound of a cork being drawn from a bottle—a sound made with a pop-gun!

Meanwhile, in London, Marconi had prepared a studio which was to launch the most famous broadcasting station in British broadcasting history—2 LO. 'Studio' is perhaps too luxurious a description: when the first broadcast went out from 2 LO on 11 May 1922, it was from the cinema theatre on the top floor of Marconi House, over microphones which were substantially the same as those used in conventional telephones.

At first 2 LO was allowed to broadcast only between 11 and 12 am, or between 2 and 4 pm, and there was to be no music. Within a month or so, music was allowed and, by June, the station was broadcasting regular 'musical evenings'. Listeners did not find them very satisfactory, and that familiar item of BBC archives the 'listeners' complaints' file was opened. Listeners could not hear properly, or one instrument sounded like another, or the music was too loud, or too soft, or too familiar, or too unfamiliar. Remarks like, 'Thank God that's over!' were made by some nervous performers, and sailed onto the air; others fell over the leads which covered the studio floor (the noun 'wireless' has always been a misnomer!). And despite enormous care, the Marconi Company were accused by the *Daily Mail* of using radio for 'political purposes'.

Some of those early broadcasts—organised by Arthur Burrows, later to become the BBC's first Director of Pro-grammes—were extremely ambitious. The very first one was a commentary on a prize-fight between Kid Lewis and Georges Carpentier. In October 1922 there came the first royal broad-cast, in which the Prince of Wales spoke to boy scouts from a rally at Alexandra Palace. This last broadcast had an enormous effect: for the first time some newspapers began to publish in advance the times at which programmes could be heard, and specialist radio journals began to multiply—among them *The Broadcaster* and *Amateur Wireless*. (The latter had a circulation of 100,000 by 1924.)

Marconi was not the only company broadcasting in 1922: there was the Manchester Metrovick station, 2 ZY, Western Electric's 2 WP station in London and its 5 IT station in Birmingham. But everyone was gradually recognising that a plethora of stations, all broadcasting at once and uncorrelated, would fill the air with undisciplined cacophany, and events were moving towards one step: the formation of the British Broadcasting Company.

The BBC was formed on 18 October 1922, at a meeting in London attended by representatives of over 200 firms connected in one way or another with radio. The Company aimed to obtain from the Postmaster General a licence which would permit it to set up stations to broadcast 'news, information, concerts, lectures, educational matter, speeches, weather reports, theatrical entertainment, and any other matter permitted.'

There was a great deal of discussion before the licence was granted: particularly over the matter of the presentation of news. The powerful newspaper proprietors saw in radio news programmes a severe threat to the circulation of their papers—particularly of the London evening papers. And then there was also the matter of finance. But the BBC obtained its licence on 18 January 1923, and broadcasting began on a regular basis.

By that time, the Company had a General Manager: a Scot—one Mr J. C. W. Reith, the son of a clergyman, thirty-four years old, and the ex-General Manager of an engineering firm. He had seen an advertisement in the Press asking for applicants for the post of General Manager of the BBC, attended an interview, and was offered the post at £1,750 a year. Accepting, he wrote in his diary: 'I am profoundly thankful to God for His goodness in this matter. It is all His doing.'

That religious note was one which was to accompany all his activities at the BBC until, in 1938, he walked weeping through the doors of Broadcasting House, having resigned his Director Generalship. His diaries, recently published, have revealed him as a bitter, disappointed man, envious and ungrateful. But whatever criticisms may be made of his personality, of the great part he played in the establishment of broadcasting in Great Britain there can surely be no argument. He set up rules of morality which now seem outrageously strict, even by the standards of his own time—but they at least had the effect of making the BBC the trusted body it was—infinitely more trusted than was the most respectable newspaper by its readers.

His policy of giving listeners what he felt they should have, rather than what they wanted, may be seen by some as indefensible: but the result was that the BBC educated its listeners until they became arguably the best informed public of any country in the Western world. His policy in music alone led to a truly vast interest in, and audience for, classical music. Paternalistic he may have been; but he was in many ways not a bad parent.

Reith worked himself into the ground during the first few weeks of the BBC, and saw to it that most other people did too. His office was on the second floor of the General Electric Company's office in Kingsway. Soon, he had six telephones installed, and was working twelve hours a day. He was not alone—and was told by one of his assistants that if conditions did not ease up, he would have a breakdown.

'You might let me know when you're going to have it,' he replied, 'then we can take turns.'

Reith not only had to organise the Company and supervise its broadcasts, but also combat the considerable opposition to broadcasting. We may think now that the world welcomed radio with open arms, but that was not the case—any more than the great television boom was to be welcomed unreservedly, years later. Radio would close all the theatres, keep people out of the cinemas, all social intercourse would cease, bridge parties would be disturbed, good conversation would be a thing of the past, and the Vicar would no longer get an audience for the Church Concert. People would stop thinking for themselves and only think what 'the wireless' told them to think; they would lose their regional accents, and all talk alike. . . .

The *Radio Times* (first issued on 28 September 1923) did its best to counter some of these accusations. Radio, it argued, would keep husbands at home in the evenings, would make music readily available to those who could not go to concerts, would bring the news to listeners some time earlier than the most speedily circulated newspapers; minds would be opened and horizons enlarged.

By the end of 1924, Reith had a staff of about 400 to control; and it grew by 150 within the next year. Every one of them, including the office boys, was at first personally interviewed by the General Manager. As the staff grew, so did the listening figures. Almost 2,000 letters a day were arriving at the offices by 1924. Two provincial stations were also operating outside London—in Manchester and Birmingham (whence *Children's Hour* was first broadcast, in 1923).

Most of the early broadcasts from 2 LO had come from a tiny cupboard of a studio in Magnet House, near Kingsway. But in

Radio Times, September 28, 1923.

THE OFFICIAL ORGAN OF THE B.B.C.

Vol. 1. No. 1. [Registered at the G.P.O. as a Newspaper.]   EVERY FRIDAY.   Two Pence.

OFFICIAL PROGRAMMES

OF

THE BRITISH BROADCASTING COMPANY.

For the Week Commencing
SUNDAY, SEPTEMBER 30th.

LONDON   CARDIFF
BIRMINGHAM   NEWCASTLE
MANCHESTER   GLASGOW

SPECIAL CONTENTS:

LORD GAINFORD'S MESSAGE TO LISTENERS.

P. P. ECKERSLEY ON "SIMULTANEOUS BROADCASTING."

A SONG OF ANCIENT CHINA.

GOSSIP ABOUT ARTISTES.

WIRELESS HUMOUR.

THE "UNCLES'" CORNER.

LETTERS FROM LISTENERS.

WHAT'S IN THE AIR?
By ARTHUR R. BURROWS, Director of Programmes.

HULLO, EVERYONE!
We will now give you *The Radio Times*. The good *new* times. The Bradshaw of Broadcasting.

May you never be late for your favourite wave-train.

Speed 186,000 miles per second; five-hour non-stops.

Family season ticket: First Class, 10s. per year.

* * * *

[*All this, presumably, is "by the way" i not "In the Air."*—EDITOR.]

* * *

So I am instructed to write about programmes and not "talk like an Uncle"!

* * *

Let me tell you all about our plans.

Wait, though! I—I'm just a little bit uneasy. My predecessor in the broadcasting business made a mistake of this character with painful consequences.

You probably remember the incident.

A Company, with distinguished Directors, having lofty ambitions, established a power-station at Westminster. Despite quite a stirring programme there were no oscillations, owing to Government intervention. The Director (Guido Fawkes) and his colleagues somehow lost their heads, and the long-anticipated report failed to materialize.

When WE broadcast Parliament—and it's bound to happen this century or next—the process will be a more dignified one than that planned in 1605. The fate of the culprits may be another matter.

* * *

Perhaps, after all, it is by stepping clear of the pitfalls of ancient and modern history that British broadcasting has got so far without any serious mishap. (Touch wood!)

* * *

Do you know that from November 14th last year until now, with only six out of eight projected stations in operation, and despite oppo-

sition from some of the "Big Noises" in the entertainment industry, we have shaken the ether of Great Britain for approximately 8,000 hours and have transmitted roughly 1,700 distinct evening programmes. How this ether-shaking process has been carried through so uninterruptedly is for my unrepentant colleague, Captain Eckersley, to tell (possibly with Morse and reactive obligato). The fact remains that if our plans for the next twelve months go through, even in their present basic form, we shall add to this record 2,500 other distinct programmes, consisting of 16,500 hours of ever-changing musical, dramatic, and instructive entertainment.

[Foulsham & Banfield.] [Photo]
Mr. ARTHUR R. BURROWS.

* * *

Two thousand five hundred distinct programmes!

[*Perhaps it IS as well that your comments are inaudible.*]

And some folk pressing for a six-hour day!

* * *

Have you ever played jigsaw?

At 2, Savoy Hill, London, W.C.2, is the biggest jigsaw puzzle yet invented, railway time-tables *not* excepted. It goes by the name of simultaneous broadcasting, a process which comes into existence so far as our musical programmes are concerned on Monday next, October 1st. For some weeks now the writer and others of the same Department, all in varying states of mental distress, have pored over this latest brain-teaser, trying to coax a refractory twiddly-bit into some time-space for which it was never intended.

(Continued in column 3, page 2)

April 1923 new studios were opened at Savoy Hill, overlooking the river, and next to the Savoy Hotel. Until 1931, Savoy Hill was to be the home of the BBC, and radio history was to be made there—at what Gale Pedrick, one of the pioneers, was to call 'quite the most pleasant club in London'.

The Institute of Electrical Engineers occupied a large building at Savoy Hill, and Reith had learned that there might be some spare room there. After a quiet look round, he rented part of the building and, by 1 May, a tiny attic studio (known for some reason as Studio Three) was opened under the roof. Into it moved the broadcasters, and from it came 2 LO's announcements, news bulletins, talks and music—even orchestras and choruses squashed into Studio Three in the early days.

Because of the somewhat rudimentary microphones in use, Studio Three and its later companions were heavily carpeted and hung with thick curtains: singers, especially, were surprised

Tommy Handley and friend (Heather Thatcher) confront one of the most solid of 'meat-safe' microphones in a heavily draped studio at Savoy Hill

(left)
The first issue (23 September 1923) of *The Radio Times*, in due course to have more readers than any other periodical ever produced in England, carried the BBC's guide to its programmes, as well as notes on broadcasters and official propaganda

and worried to be entirely deprived of the normal timbre of their voices, and found themselves shouting and forcing their tone in an attempt to deal with the 'dead' acoustics.

Studio One was open within a month or two: a larger room into which military bands and large orchestras fitted somewhat more comfortably—though the word 'comfort' is relative, for the ventilation was appalling; fans had to be turned off during broadcasts, because of the noise they made and the fact that when ducts were open listeners were disturbed by the hooting of Thames tugs or pleasure craft.

All this was in the Institute's west wing (Reith's own office looked out across Embankment Gardens to Waterloo Bridge). In 1924, the BBC also moved into the northern wing, looking out onto the Savoy Chapel. After rebuilding the piece of the north-west corner of the block which had been bombed by a passing zeppelin, and gutting some flats which had formed another part of the wing, the Company built itself four more studios, and eventually ended up with a total of seven, including one two storeys high, of which Reith was particularly proud.

The whole building was friendly if idiosyncratic—it was visited each evening by a little man in search of rodents in the old fabric ('Any mice, please?' he would call through open office doors). Office boys in rubber gloves circulated to fill up the inkwells, others puffed germicide over staff and visitors alike (broadcasters lived in mortal fear of coughs and sneezes). Instructions on how, and when, and with what to gargle were circularised.

While Reith stalked the corridors, the announcers and engineers were more concerned with the studios. Technically, they seem to have been (to say the least) limited. These were the days of the 'meat-safe' microphone—or the Round-Sykes Magnetophone, to give it its proper title. It was slung in sponge rubber mounted in a square wooden frame covered with silk, and wheeled about on a sturdy tripod. Containing a magnet strong enough to stop any watch brought near it, it was in some respects over-sensitive: for the benefit of the inexperienced broadcaster a notice in Gothic type announced that, 'If you cough or rustle your papers, you will deafen millions of listeners.' Sometimes such an occurrence would put the micro-phone out of order for some time, and there would be a silent interval while another was fitted. When, during a broadcast about his day's work, a Post Office employee describing the night mail suddenly took it into his head to blow a whistle, the transmitter went off the air for forty-five minutes, and repairs cost £350. Norman Long, the comedian, used to carry a nasal spray, which frequently drowned the sound of the other artistes' voices. Once the voices had been successfully captured through the microphone, there were still occasional difficulties, as when, on 31 May 1925, 2 LO was off the air for nineteen minutes owing to the intervention of an adventurous mouse, which found its way into a high-capacity condenser in the transmitter set up on the top of Selfridge's in Oxford Street.

For the most part, however, the somewhat Heath-Robinsonian equipment managed to launch the sound waves into the innocent air, and they found their way to the eager listener's ten-and-sixpenny 'Brownie' wireless crystal set (giving 'clear-toned voluminous reception' over a radius of thirty miles), or later to the luxurious Philips Radio Type 634-A (at sixteen guineas), perhaps via Captain S. R. Mullard's HF Double Red Ring valves. There were other, splendidly eccentric, receivers, including one in the shape of a rosebowl, guaranteed to work equally well whether empty or full of flowers!

But what were the sounds that eventually reached the ear of the listener? Comparatively little broadcasting went on in those early days—some schools' programmes in the afternoons,

The Savoy Orpheans Band, photographed in 1924 (note the microphone hanging from the lampshade). The personnel of the band changed constantly, but in the early days Billy Mayerl, Bert Ralton and George Eckdale were all members

some teatime music, and dance-music from the conveniently neighbouring Savoy Hotel in the evening—Stuart Hibberd and his fellow-announcers closing down the studio at 10.30 pm, quickly changing into evening dress, and popping into the hotel just in time to announce the numbers to be played by the Savoy Orpheans or the Savoy Havana Band, and to enjoy a welcome snack provided by the grateful management in a back room.

A little later, De Groot and his Piccadilly Hotel Orchestra, and Albert Sandler and his Grand Hotel Orchestra from Eastbourne, became popular with a less frenetic type of music; *Grand Hotel*, directly inspired by those early broadcasts, survived into the 1970s, and for years revolved around a central medley of tunes from new musicals just presented in London, giving one one's first opportunity of hearing them in the days before hit tunes from new shows were plugged for months before opening night.

It is not generally realised today that it was not until the outbreak of World War II that the BBC was regularly allowed to broadcast news programmes before 7 pm. On the insistence of the newspaper managements, it was mid-evening before Mr Hibberd was allowed to go to the microphone and announce: 'This is London calling—2 LO calling. Here is the first general news bulletin, copyright by Reuter, Press Association, Exchange Telegraph and Central News.' Then came a staid, solemn news bulletin collated from the tapes of the various news agencies. No news interviews, no news features, no actuality. It was all a very skeletal affair.

But despite the difficulties and restrictions, a few people were already beginning to make their names and reputations 'on the air'. 'Wireless Willie' (a comedian called Willie Rous) was one of them; 'Our Lizzie' (Helene Millais) another; and perhaps the best known of all, John Henry, the Yorkshire comedian, who, with his wife Blossom, became as celebrated as the comparatively small audience of listeners allowed.

'Talks' formed a large part of radio diet: a term which covered every kind of verbal broadcast from interviews with the famous—Tom Mix in stetson and spurs, or Will Rogers, among others—to descriptions of theatrical first nights, from advice on gardening to autobiographical reminiscences. Reith was particularly careful that people coming to the microphone (as well as, of course, his announcers) should make proper use of the English language—BBC English was to become famous, and later almost infamous; it had disadvantages as well as advantages, no doubt. But at any event, English usage was guarded by an Advisory Committee on Spoken English, members of which included the Poet Laureate, Robert Bridges, Rudyard Kipling, Logan Pearsall-Smith (an American educated at Harvard and Oxford), and Bernard Shaw. Among the first things they considered was the verb *to broadcast* and the noun *listener*. Should programmes be *broadcast* or *broadcasted*? Were those who heard them *listeners* or *listeners-in*? Reith decided that 'a listener' was someone who had paid for his receiving licence, and therefore heard words addressed to him. A 'listener-in' was a man who had not paid his fee, and therefore overheard the broadcasts!

The radio talks themselves were from the beginning extremely varied. There were regular features: literary criticism from John Strachey, musical talks by Percy Scholes, discussion of films by G. A. Atkinson, and of the theatre by Archibald Haddon, succeeded in 1925 by James Agate, perhaps the most influential critic of his generation.

Looking back, perhaps the most reputable broadcaster of the early 1920s was a storyteller who made his first broadcast—a story called *My Adventures in Jermyn Street*—in January 1924. He was a civil servant, Leslie Lambert, and he called himself A. J. Alan. He broadcast irregularly and infrequently, whetting the audience's appetite by making it clear that he used a pseudonym, but steadfastly refusing any personal publicity (it was only after his death in 1940 that his true name became known).

Alan would appear in the studio dressed in a dinner-jacket (even before the days when announcers were ordered to wear them), and from a neat black brief-case produce his script and a candle, in case the lights fused. Then, adjusting his eyeglass, he would lift himself onto a high stool near the 'meat-safe' and speak quietly into it in a carefully modulated voice—it is said that he neither smoked nor drank for at least a week before broadcasting.

Alan was in a sense the first man to make his reputation as a truly professional broadcaster. Even the early announcers learned their craft by a combination of trial and error, and many performers were overcome with terror in the unfamiliar atmosphere of the studio—Tallulah Bankhead actually collapsed in a faint on the floor after a Week's Good Cause appeal. But Alan seemed to have grasped the true nature of the medium from the beginning. He pasted his scripts to pieces of cardboard so that they could never rustle or crackle, spoiling the illusion of an *ad lib* story. To help the illusion still further, he would mark his scripts like a conductor's score—'cough', 'pause', 'breath heavily'.

Most professional broadcasters who started their careers in

the Savoy Hill days have paid tribute to Alan as the supreme professional; and some of them shared his *punctilio*. Commenting on the rule (established in January 1926) that all announcers should change into black tie in the evenings, Stuart Hibberd has said that he 'always thought it right and proper that announcers should wear evening dress on duty', though the disadvantages included the fact that the engineers occasionally had to warn him that his starched shirt-front was creaking during the news bulletin.

This formalism was much to John Reith's taste, and it was he, with his Scottish Presbyterian upbringing, who introduced the idea of broadcast prayers to close the day's radio on Sunday evenings (though in the 1920s any director of broadcasting would probably have done the same). At first, the duty announcer simply read a few verses from the Old or New Testament, chosen by J. C. Stobart, the BBC's Education Director, one of whose hobbies was the composition of light verse in Latin or Greek. Later, a hymn, psalm, or a sacred song was added, and the London Station Director, Rex Palmer, would render *Abide with Me* or *Nearer, my God, to Thee*.

Eventually, *The Epilogue*, first broadcast under that title in 1926, became an extremely popular programme, and prominent MPs were among members of the audience who requested that details of it should be printed in the *Radio Times*—leading to the splendid announcement, a cutting of which Stuart Hibberd carried around in his pocket-book for years:

> 10.30 pm. The Epilogue.
> The Commandments.
> 'Thou shalt not commit Adultery.'
> (For details see page 140).

Religion was no laughing matter, however—neither for Reith nor his carefully chosen first lieutenants. They were all of the same mind: that since England was a Christian country, and the Church of England the established Church, religious broadcasts must form an important part of the broadcast diet.

The *Daily Service* was instituted in 1928, and warmly greeted. Among the many letters of congratulation, the following, quoted in the 1930 *BBC Yearbook*, is revealing:

> We suggested to the maids that they should come in if they wished, and now, for several months, the family and the maids and gardener meet in the dining-room at 10.15 and take part in the service. We always stand for the Lord's Prayer and the Gloria, and join in the singing when we can.

It was at this time too that the BBC Drama Department began its tradition of presenting new as well as classical plays—a tradition among the most satisfactory and admirable of all the Corporation's hereditary glories.

The first piece of drama to be broadcast was the quarrel scene from *Julius Caesar*, played by Robert Atkins and Basil Gill. Atkins was to become an adept radio performer; but it was the policy of theatre managements to deny the BBC the right to broadcast excerpts from current plays, and many actors found themselves disqualified from giving radio performances while they were appearing in the West End. Still, distinguished theatre people found their way to Savoy Hill: Lewis Casson produced several plays as early as 1924, and his wife, Sybil Thorndike, broadcast with him in *Medea* very early in radio history. Between August 1924 and September 1925, 149 drama productions were broadcast from Savoy Hill, with casts including many reputable players of the day—Lady Forbes Robertson, Mrs Kendall, Lady Tree, Gladys Cooper. . . . Over 900 auditions were held for actors who wanted to work in the medium. The Company made the decision to present the listener with as realistic a 'theatrical' experience as possible, even going as far as to play a four- or five-minute overture before performances began.

During the war, Dame Sybil Thorndike broadcast a programme in the series 'My Life in the Theatre'; at the microphone with her are her husband, Lewis Casson, and her daughter Ann

In the 1920s, radio, the novelty of the age, was used to entice people into shops and restaurants,—even on to trains: it is on a train that these four solemn businessmen are listening to the crackling sound emerging from an early horned wireless set

Radio drama had some way to go before it found its feet. Technical resources were pretty bald: experiments with sound effects were adventurous and often unsuccessful. When an early play demanded the sound of a shot, the first BBC Drama Director, R. E. Jeffrey, fired a real shot-gun down the staircase well outside the studio. The noise sounded, it is reported, like the opening of a rather flat bottle of champagne!

Many of our most admired contemporary playwrights were to start their careers in radio, and it should be recorded that the first play specifically commissioned for radio from a professional author was *The White Chateau*, by Reginald Berkeley, which was broadcast on Armistice Day 1925.

Drama was not confined to theatrical performances. On 16 April 1925, the celebrated Roman Catholic preacher Ronald Knox made a sensation which (allowing for the relative size of the audience) might be compared to that provoked in America in 1938 by Orson Welles' famous adaptation of H. G. Wells' *The War of the Worlds*. Fr Knox described a revolution allegedly

occurring in England, with the roasting alive of a well known financier in Trafalgar Square, and the pelting of the ducks in the Serpentine with ginger-beer bottles. Many listeners took *Broadcasting the Barricades* perfectly seriously, and Stuart Hibberd, on duty at Savoy Hill, had to answer many letters of enquiry and complaint, including one from a commercial traveller who had arrived home to find his wife and sister-in-law terrified and somewhat incoherent, and an empty brandy bottle under the table nearby.

Children's Hour was the first regular programme of its length —forty-five minutes—to be broadcast by the BBC; it became enormously popular, two generations of Englishmen and women grew up with it, and its influence was quite incalculable until it was slaughtered after the war to be replaced by a news magazine programme.

Children's Hour at first involved almost everybody in the BBC. Indeed, it was at first almost a King Charles' head. Reith was extremely involved in it, seeing the Company's daily programme

Children's Hour, one of the first regular programmes to be broadcast by the BBC, at first engaged the attention of spare-time performers—announcers became the first 'uncles' and 'aunts'. But by the 1940s, when this photograph was taken, professional actors and producers gave it the serious attention which made it one of the most professional of programmes

for children as, 'a happy alternative to the squalor of streets and back yards.' It seems in retrospect that more attention was paid to this programme than almost any other; the most staid announcers and members of staff became 'uncles' and 'aunties' —some of them, Uncle Caractacus, Uncle Arthur, Auntie Phyllis or Auntie Sophie, becoming personal friends of thousands of children.

Under Mrs Ella Fitzgerald, Central Organiser of Children's Hour, Auntie Geraldine and Uncle Peter and the rest saw to the running of a gigantic children's party of the air—until, in 1926, it was decided that more dignity and less involvement should be the rule, and 'uncles' and 'aunties' disappeared from the pages of *Radio Times* (though not from the children's letters).

Children's Hour pioneered some broadcasts: the first play written specifically for radio was one by 'Uncle Arthur' Burrows; the first storytelling was for children; the first broadcast orchestral piece played by a BBC band was Roger Quilter's *Children's Overture*. ... Though there was some criticism from children, there was much more praise; though some teachers believed radio to be a disconcertingly popular form of education, and probably for that reason to be mistrusted, more welcomed it as opening out new worlds in the imagination. ('I like the wireless better than the theatre,' one London child wrote in a now legendary letter, 'because the scenery is better.')

Music saturated the soundwaves in the 1920s and '30s. As early as January 1923, a performance of Mozart's *The Magic Flute* had been broadcast direct from the Royal Opera House, Covent Garden, in a performance by the British National Opera Company. There was enormous interest in this event throughout the musical world; a new kind of microphone had been devised, and produced clearer sound, so that listeners all over the country heard the opera with great pleasure. 'From north, south, east and west came messages of delight over the old-fashioned telephone', wrote the *Daily Express*.

Outside broadcasts continued. But members of the BNOC and the Carl Rosa Company also came into the studio and, in 1925, broadcast the first studio performance of an opera—Bizet's *Carmen*.

Percy Pitt, the BBC's first music adviser, encouraged the formation of a BBC orchestra and, in 1923, broadcast a Wagner programme played by a band of forty musicians. After he had become Director of Music in 1924, he organised its amalgamation with the Covent Garden Orchestra, and Elgar, Richard Strauss and Siegfried Wagner were among the eminent conductors to direct it.

There was also chamber music, and there were extremely ambitious musical projects leading in the general direction of such splendid pioneering work as the broadcasting, before the war, of all Bach's cantatas. This high seriousness was not appreciated by everyone: a violinist arriving at a railway station with only a few minutes to go before he was due to play in a broadcast concert hailed a taxi. 'Savoy Hill, quickly!' he cried.

'You a musician?' asked the taxi-driver phlegmatically.

'Yes.'

'You playing in them cantatas?'

'Yes, I am.'

'Walk!' said the taxi-driver, sweeping off.

Even in those early days, 'light music'—the 'pop' of its day—was taken sufficiently seriously. Jack Hylton broadcast a discussion with Sir Landon Ronald, Principal of the Guildhall School of Music, about the relative merits of popular and classical music. George Gershwin came to the studio to play *Rhapsody in Blue* with Carroll Gibbons and the Orpheans. (He was in London for the production of *Lady be Good*, with

Carroll Gibbons led the Savoy Hotel Orpheans at the Savoy Hotel in 1932, after a legal wrangle to protect the band's name, which other ensembles had been stealing

27

the Astaires, and made some commercial gramophone records, on one of which, the label proudly announced, could be heard 'the actual sound of Fred Astaire dancing', and some incoherent words of encouragement shouted from dancer to pianist and back again—the only recording, I believe, of Gershwin's voice.)

Incidentally, the sound of dancing was quite often broadcast: there is an evocative photograph of the chorus of *Radio Radiance*, an early revue, hoofing it enthusiastically in front of a microphone; and a film of life at the BBC made some years later showed Brian Michie munching an apple and rehearsing a dancing chorus-line in the concert-hall of Broadcasting House.

Within a remarkably short period of time, it had become clear that broadcasting was the mass medium of its time, and far too important to be left to the broadcasters—or so some politicians and businessmen felt. The Crawford Committee, the first of several Government committees on the future of broadcasting, was set up in 1925, and interested parties put their various views on the conduct of radio in the coming years.

The Committee published its conclusions in March 1926. In July, the Postmaster General announced that its recommendations were accepted by the Government. Parliament's decision was based on various arguments, some publicly deployed, some kept rather quiet: Tory MPs liked the idea of authority embodied in a monopoly; Labour MPs disliked private enterprise, and though suspicious of the Company's attitude during the General Strike, at least saw that Reith had defended independence. Tories, again, thought it wise to support the setting-up of a monopoly which would be in a position to resist the wilder ideas of a Labour Government—then a distinct possibility.

At all events, the decision was made—a momentous one, only reversed with the coming of commercial television a quarter of a century later. On 31 December 1926, the British Broadcasting Company ceased to exist and was replaced by the British Broadcasting Corporation. It had a Chairman, a Vice-Chairman and a Board of Governors. But there was no doubt who remained in charge.

John Reith—to be knighted in 1927—was now presiding over a rapidly growing organisation, with a rapidly growing audience. At the end of 1922, he had had a staff of four; by the end of 1926, of over 600. In 1922, almost 26,000 people possessed radio licences; in 1926, the figure had risen to over two million, and goodness knows how many people listened without licences. New and advanced 'wireless sets' were by now on the market: for almost £50 you could buy the splendid Wootophone Four Valve Cabinet Receiver, equipped with 'aerial tuner inductances', 'serial variometers', 'geared condensers', 'coil mounts', 'anode coils', 'basket coil holders' and other mysterious niceties. Or for rather less, there was the Pye Portable—and at the bottom end of the market, you could still get 'Dr Cecil's *Real* Hertzite Crystal, Price 6d Box (Solid Silver Non-slip Whisker Free, Ensuring Perfect and Loud Reception)'.

While the wireless was being developed and then mass-produced, the Company had taken its listeners from Chelmsford and Whittle to Magnet House and Savoy Hill. Now the Corporation was to move onward and upward, towards Portland Place and Broadcasting House.

II Savoy Hill

At Christmas, 1927—just twelve months after the British Broadcasting Company had become the British Broadcasting Corporation—the *Radio Times*, the BBC's own weekly programme paper, announced that it had sold over one million copies during the past year. Within the next ten years, its circulation was to grow to over three million. It was a reflection of a decade during which radio was to become the most important medium of news and entertainment for most people in Great Britain.

The BBC took broadcasting very seriously. In contrast to the ratings mania of the 1970s, in the 1930 *Yearbook* the listener was invited to 'give the wireless a rest now and then'. And when he did listen, it must be

> as carefully . . . as in a theatre or concert hall. You can't get the best out of a programme if your mind is wandering, or if you are playing bridge or reading. Give it your full attention. Try turning out the lights . . . your imagination will be twice as vivid.

In the first issue of the *BBC Handbook*, published early in 1928, the Earl of Clarendon, Chairman of the Board of Governors, marvelled that 'in so short a space of time this new Public Service should have become so essential and powerful a factor in our life.' In his Introduction to the *Handbook*, Reith (now named Director General) struck his customary solemn note, but underlined in his own way the fact that it was part of the policy of the BBC to provide 'relaxation': 'Mitigation of the strain of a high-pressure life, such as the last generation scarcely knew, is a primary social necessity, and that necessity must be satisfied.'

'OBs'—outside broadcasts—started remarkably early in the history of radio. Sometimes they took place under hazardous conditions; sometimes just uncomfortable ones. Here, John Arlott mops his brow during a cricket commentary

Another OB—from a water-bus on the Thames. The interviewer is Wynford Vaughan Thomas, not long returned from war

Among the broadcasts designed to entertain and relax listeners, the BBC's first ventures into sports commentary were necessarily a little shaky. On 27 May 1925, there was an attempt to broadcast the sound of the horses galloping round Tattenham Corner during the Derby. Unfortunately, it was a wet day, the ground was soaked, and the going so soft that listeners heard only a series of faint plops, and Stuart Hibberd spent his afternoon in the studio apologising for a fiasco. Still, someone did shout the name of the winner 'near enough to the microphone for it to be clearly heard' (Hibberd noted in his diary); so all was not lost.

During those early days, when there was still much opposition from the Press to all news reports on radio, there were even protests that the Derby winner's name had been broadcast (the BBC argued that it was simply some chance passerby who happened to be calling out the horse's name to a chum some distance away, and that it was most unfortunate that the microphone had picked up his remark). In 1927, there was a more ambitious broadcast from Epsom, when a commentator, George Allison, wearing a 'mask microphone' (fixed firmly over the mouth to exclude extraneous noises) was held over the side of the roof of the Club Stand by a colleague, to describe the activity

in the unsaddling enclosure sixty feet below. Less arduous was the task of the commentator engaged for another sporting outside broadcast—of a hand of bridge played by Viscount Massereene, Viscount Castlerose, the Countess of Ossery and Viscountess Massereene.

That same year, Gerald Cock, Director of Outside Broadcasts, achieved a number of spectacular 'firsts': the BBC was now allowed for the first time to broadcast full commentaries on sports events, and in mid-January there was a description of a rugby match, followed closely by a soccer match commentary. The Grand National, the Boat Race, the Amateur Golf Championship and Wimbledon (at which a commentator was J. C. Squire, poet, critic, anthologist and Editor of the *London Mercury*) were also covered. In 1928 the BBC improved its Outside Broadcast service with a first OB lorry, with 'a studio compartment' and no less than six microphone points, and several very familiar names were involved in commentaries —Freddie Grisewood, Howard Marshall and John Snagge among others. Several of them were simply staff announcers, and knew very little about the games on which they had to report: Snagge broadcast the first soccer commentary (on a game between Corinthians and Newcastle United), but admitted

Early OBs took place from makeshift studios, or simply from the back of an available lorry. Here, engineers prepare for broadcasting the Derby of 1923

In 1931, a select few took to the air to view the boat-race from an air-liner: and the ubiquitous 'wireless' provided the commentary

years later that he only vaguely recognised some players, and though he could tell when a goal had been scored, that was about all. Listeners soon recognised this, and sent in several suggestions for improving the coverage of sports commentaries— among them a proposal that the referee should be engaged to describe the game as it went on around him. A microphone could be strapped to his chest, attached by an elastic lead to terminals at one of the goalposts, in order to cause him the minimum of inconvenience.

A brief look through the list of notable broadcasts during 1927 reveals instantly the increased scope of outside events covered by radio, and the scope of talks and entertainment offered. In January there was a chamber concert from France, Mendelssohn's *Hymn of Praise* from Northwich Cathedral, a debate between Bernard Shaw and G. K. Chesterton, and a birthday programme in honour of Delius. February saw the first broadcast of a Royal Variety Command Performance; March, a performance of *Peer Gynt* from Liverpool, Elgar's *Apostles* from Cardiff, an experiment in mass telepathy conducted by Sir Oliver Lodge, and Beethoven's *Mass in D* from the Albert

Hall (marking the centenary of Beethoven's death).

And so the list goes on. What the BBC did not note in detail in its *Yearbook* was the more 'normal' day-to-day entertainment: among which, during the 1920s and early 1930s, dance music was probably more popular than anything else. The dance craze was at its height between the two world wars, and while the 1930s probably saw the apogee of dance-band music, it was in the late 1920s that bands began to impress their individuality on the public—to some extent through a growing number of gramophone recordings, but chiefly through broadcasting although, occasionally, the nonconformist hand of Reith seems to be seen gesturing irritably in the direction of this popular, almost cult, entertainment. In 1934, for instance, an edict was issued forbidding the use of the phrase 'hot music', and banning scat singing. The *Melody Maker* published a cartoon showing Auntie BBC spanking a boy labelled 'Listening Public', with the words: 'There, brat! Whether you like it or not, your mind's got to be elevated!'

The first dance band to broadcast in Great Britain was Marius B. Winter's group, heard from the attic studios of

OB units not only broadcast the excitements of sport, but more rural delights: here, engineers prepare to attempt to broadcast the song of the nightingale

Marconi House on 23 March 1923. A year later, Mr Winter was heard on Radio Paris, and so became the first bandleader to broadcast on commercial radio! He later claimed also to have been the first bandleader to use a signature tune, but though all this may be true, he is all but forgotten today. The Savoy Orpheans are not.

No doubt if the BBC had been set up in studios elsewhere in London, the Savoy Hotel would not have played such an enormous role in the broadcasting of dance music. As it was, the convenience of simply running a line next door was overwhelming, and it was as early as April 1923 that the first live broadcast of dance music from the Savoy was heard: the band was the Savoy Havana, led by Bert Ralton, an American saxophonist. They were appearing at the hotel at the time, in succession to several other groups which had played for dancing there, off and on, since 1916.

At the end of 1923 Bert Ralton left England, and the Savoy Orpheans Band was formed by Debroy Somers who, four years later, was succeeded as leader by Carroll Gibbons. As a result of its popularity with listeners, it made many recordings and took part in some rather strange concerts, including a 'Symphonic Syncopation' concert at the Queen's Hall in which it joined forces with the visiting Boston Orchestra: the programme included *Wagneria* and *Chaliapinata* as well as *Beale Street Blues*.

Another band playing at the Savoy which made many radio 'appearances' was Fred Elizalde's. Elizalde brought his group to the Savoy in 1927, to play opposite the Orpheans; but there were many complaints from dancers, for Elizande was a controversially *avant-garde* musician, and it was extremely difficult actually to dance to much of his music. 'Lizz' declined to play simple waltzes and foxtrots; and criticism of the kind of music he did play—well ahead of its time—was not confined to the dancers: listeners wrote to complain to the BBC that his music 'had no tunes'. They were not so far out. Elizalde had, after all, said that to him 'melody is an entirely secondary consideration as far as dance music is concerned'.

Radio established the reputations of a large number of bands and bandleaders outside the Savoy Hotel. The first OB of a dance band from another London hotel was by Ben Davis' Carlton House Dance Band (in May 1923). A year later, Henry Hall made his first broadcast with the Gleneagles Hotel Orchestra. Jack Payne and the Hotel Cecil Orchestra were regularly heard, and in February 1926 came the first BBC house band—the London Radio Dance Band, under Sidney Firman, which played regularly at the Cavour Restaurant.

Lew Stone was another important radio bandleader, who worked incessantly (very often sixteen to eighteen hours a day). He had formed a band in 1932 to play at the Monseigneur Restaurant, and soon began broadcasting regularly in place of Roy Fox. Later he moved to other restaurants, but remained a regular broadcaster for the next thirty-five years.

Roy Fox, whose illness gave Lew Stone his chance, was an American who came to London in 1930 for a season at the Café de Paris. He had only been broadcasting from the Monseigneur for eighteen months when illness removed him from the scene and, by the time he had recovered, Lew Stone was too firmly esconced in the affection of patrons and listeners to allow him to return there. He formed another band, and was heard regularly on the air until he went to Australia in 1938.

The third of the great bandleaders of the 1930s was Ambrose —Bert Ambrose, a Londoner who had studied in New York, returned to London to play at the Embassy Club in Bond Street, and in 1927 was appointed Musical Director at the Mayfair Hotel at the then staggering salary of £10,000 a year. He first broadcast from the Mayfair on 20 March 1928, and fortnightly from then on—though he was one of the bandleaders who refused to broadcast during the time the Corporation banned announcements and vocals. When the ban was lifted, he had a regular 10.30 to midnight programme every Saturday evening— the star spot of the week, which gave him an extraordinary following throughout the country. He went on playing—from the Mayfair, then the Embassy, then the Mayfair again, and finally from the Café de Paris—right up until the war.

These were the most notable freelance bands. There were many others: Jay Whidden's, from the Carlton, Ray Starita's (really run by Jack Hylton) from the Ambassador Club, Teddy Brown's from the Café de Paris, Debroy Somers' from Ciro's, Ronnie Munro's from the Florida, George Fisher's from the Kit-Cat, and Kettner's Five from Kettner's. They broadcast from time to time, or even regularly, but none of them were in any sense the property of the BBC.

The Corporation's own band, led by Jack Payne, was quite another matter. He had been born in Leamington Spa and, while in the Royal Flying Corps during World War I, had organised a few little groups of musicians into bands, so that when he was demobbed at the end of the war it was to popular music that he looked for a career.

In 1925, he was engaged to play with a six-piece band at the Hotel Cecil in the Strand, and when the BBC agreed to broadcast the Cecil band, he brought four more musicians in. In 1928, the BBC dance band was formed and he was engaged to lead it. The BBC *Handbook* had, it seems, some doubts, for it started its article on the formation of the new band with a sort of apology for broadcasting music which 'some people' had called 'cacophonous, monotonous, cheap, puerile, barbarous, bestial . . .'. But there was no escaping the fact that 'dance band music has been from the first one of the most popular features of the broadcast programmes', and now here was the BBC's own dance band, with its pianist (combining celesta), its tenor banjo (also adept upon the tenor guitar, Spanish guitar and tenor saxophone), its sousaphonist (capable too of splendid things upon the double bass) and its other musicians, all of them liable to give out without warning 'sounds of a vigorous and rhythmic nature'. The astute players, the *Year-book* warned, 'can get so many different noises out of a trumpet that it is quite unrecognisable as the same instrument.'

Jack Payne's BBC band played for variety programmes as well as for dance-music programmes; they even provided incidental music for plays! They became so popular that any attempt to keep up with their fan mail was useless, and printed cards of acknowledgement were used.

Jack Payne (*on the left*), formerly leader of the BBC Dance Orchestra, was catapulted by radio to such fame that he constantly chartered special trains to rush from a provincial engagement (in this case at Chatham) to the London studios

As famous as Payne, or perhaps even more so, was his successor as leader of the BBC dance band, one Henry Hall, a Clapham boy who had studied music at the Guildhall School, Trinity College, and to some extent as a member of a Salvation Army Band! He had worked as a cinema pianist during World War I, and in 1924 led the band at the Gleneagles Hotel in Perthshire. That band, of only six players, broadcast first in the year it was formed, but Henry Hall began a successful career as a bandleader without much help from radio. By 1930 he was musical director for a large group of hotels (owned by the London, Midland and Scottish Railway) controlling over thirty bands.

His first broadcast with the BBC band took place in March 1932, and in no time at all his was as big a household name as Jack Payne's. From 1934 until he left the BBC in 1937, and periodically after that, he broadcast a weekly *Guest Night*, and his rather halting personal announcement—'This *is* Henry Hall, and tonight is my Guest Night'—became a national catch-phrase in the very early years of radio catch-phrases.

Henry Hall was something of an innovator. He was not con-

Henry Hall's guest on one of his regular programmes in the '30s was the already celebrated actor-composer Noël Coward. The tight control over studio conditions maintained by Lord Reith would have ensured that Mr Coward's glass contained only water

39

Billy Cotton, whose career in radio lasted from 1928 until his death in 1969, was an excellent publicist: but he actually did drive in the Junior Car Club's International Trophy Race at Brooklands in 1938!

tent simply to take over Payne's ensemble at the BBC. His band—which, incidentally, broadcast the first piece of music ever to sound out from the new Broadcasting House in Portland Place (it was *Here's to the Next Time*)—had fourteen musicians, including (for a while, and for the first time perhaps in any dance band) an oboist. He had chosen his men from over 700 applicants for auditions. In 1933, he began making personal appearances—the first of them was at that year's Radiolympia Exhibition—and became one of the best known and best loved radio personalities of his generation.

Several bandleaders who made early broadcasts were to become familiar to BBC listeners, and some of them survived to make a name in post-war radio and television. Billy Cotton was their doyen. An extrovert character whose band broadcast regularly before World War II, but who became really famous in the 1950s with the Billy Cotton Band Show, he worked right up to within hours of his death. Charlie Kunz (the first bandleader to broadcast dance music on a Sunday!) later became known as an individual musician—in his case, as a pianist with a remarkably consistent, metronome-like beat and a bouncy rhythm which made him an enormous favourite.

If dance music was a vital part of BBC light entertainment almost from the beginning of radio broadcasting, it was some years before variety—in time to become the second most important ingredient of daily broadcasting in the early years—was possible on any scale. The trouble was the almost hysterical reaction to the coming of radio of theatre impresarios and managements. Though extracts from West End musical comedies and revues were broadcast in the very early days, the Society of West End Theatre Managers set its face against too much broadcasting of 'variety'—and had the full support of important individual managements such as Moss Empires. Very occasionally a broadcast would be allowed 'live' from a theatre: but they were few and far between until after 1925, when Walter Payne, President of the Society, was finally persuaded to sign an agreement with the BBC. He had always believed fiercely that broadcasting diminished the value of an artiste to theatre managements, but at last began to realise the truth: that though there were senses in which radio taxed a performer's ingenuity (he could no longer use one script for three or four years, touring it around the halls, but had to find new material for each broadcast) the publicity he received from radio was absolutely invaluable.

By 1931, the BBC was broadcasting over 150 variety pro-grammes a year, and did not find it easy. Part of the difficulty was, of course, that the Corporation's idea of humour was still rather more literary than music hall. 'Few comedians are capable of writing their own material', complained the *Yearbook*, 'and the dearth of clever humorous writers is even greater.' It is a complaint which has been heard at regular intervals ever since. The BBC much preferred the somewhat arcane humour of Gillie Potter (the Sage of Hogs Norton, and one of the most individual broadcasters of his time) to the music-hall humour of the more popular comedians of the halls. ('The slap-stick, red-nosed comedian is dead,' said the 1931 *Yearbook*. So much for Ken Dodd!)

Attempting to please everyone, the writer explained, the BBC recognised two types of variety (or 'vaudeville', the term preferred). One was 'the broader type of performance' which would be 'supported by dance music'; the other was much more intellectually stimulating, and might contain French or German cabaret numbers, songs from operetta, 'and generally one comedian, carefully selected'. Looking at lists of variety artistes appearing on radio during 1931, it is fairly easy to divide them into the two categories. The coarser material would no doubt come from Will Hay, Norman Long, Wee Georgie Wood, the Americans Burns and Allen, Gracie Fields

Tommy Handley paying attention to Horace Percival during a rehearsal of ITMA, in 1944

(billed as comédienne rather than singer), Florrie Forde, Sophie Tucker, Nellie Wallace and Elsie and Doris Waters, while into the second category would fall the elegant Ronald Frankau (teamed with Tommy Handley—interestingly, a large portrait of him appeared in the 1929 *Yearbook*, captioned 'a great wireless comedian'—in an act called 'Murgatroyd and Winterbottom'), Jack Hulbert, a splendid musical comedy player, Gillie Potter, Bransby Williams with his dramatic monologues and recitations, Claude Hulbert and Enid Trevor, José Collins, star of *Maid of the Mountains*, and the first musical comedy star to broadcast from 2 LO, Beatrice Lillie, a comédienne of the fashionable intelligentsia if ever there was one, the coloured singers Layton and Johnstone, and perhaps the impressionist Harry Hemsley, with his imaginary family of children, the youngest speaking a language all his own ('What did Horace say, Winnie?').

The broadcasting of variety had its production problems. (One wonders who booked a conjuror to 'appear' on the radio in 1927?) One of the most taxing was calculating the degree to which the listener at home would find the comedian's timing of his act, ruled by his 'live' audience, puzzling or irritating. Then with still more or less rudimentary microphones, there were purely technical problems. Summarising the year's variety in 1930, the *Yearbook* mentions approvingly Jackie Coogan's Palladium appearance, the sensation caused by Flotsam and Jetsam at the Alhambra, and the successful broadcast of the operetta *Cupid and the Cutlets* from the Coliseum, but regretted that Will Hay, at the Palladium, was so funny that the audience's roars of continual laughter made him inaudible to listeners at home.

Until 1930, the organisation of radio variety was a rather *ad hoc* affair. However, in that year, the Revue and Vaudeville Section of the BBC was formed, and among the results of this piece of reorganisation were broadcasts of the first radio series— *Songs from the Shows*, *Music Hall* and *The White Coons' Concert Party* (hardly a title which would appeal today).

Music Hall was a popular programme which ran for years: I remember listening to it avidly on Saturday nights before and during World War II. It took the form (as its title suggests) of a music-hall bill, with a number of 'turns' of all sorts—it might be Flanagan and Allen (two new young artistes who appeared on the show for the first time in 1932), or Anne Ziegler and Webster Booth (romantic duettists somewhat on the model of Jeannette MacDonald and Nelson Eddy). It was one of the first programmes to be broadcast with a studio audience— which meant certain concessions as to dress and even staging.

The artistes no longer appeared in casual clothing, but wore stage costume and even make-up; and the stage equipment which was needed for the first *Music Hall* had to be borrowed from the BBC Amateur Dramatic Society.

Radio revue also had a brief vogue. *Radio Radiance* was the first of them—produced in a Savoy Hill studio in 1925, it ran weekly for over a year, and its chorus, a group of girls known to announcers as 'the Miniature Suite', danced on boards in the studio to provide the aural equivalent of a chorus line. Tommy Handley made his first radio appearance in one of *Radio Radiance's* numbers. In *Winners*, a very loose running plot linked together popular musical-comedy numbers; then Ernest Longstaffe broke away with a series of programmes which took a single theme—perhaps the rush hour, or shop-lifting—and embroidered it with original music and dialogue. There was a series of radio Charlot revues, and some weak imitations such as *Peep-Bo-Hemia* and *Piccadilly Dally*.

Listeners often complained that popular musical comedies of the period were not broadcast. The chief answer was of course a simple one: the owners of the copyright would not permit it, on the familiar grounds that once the show had been heard on the radio, no-one would want to go and see it on the stage. But it is also true that BBC engineers were not very keen on OBs from theatres: there was great difficulty in getting the sound right. An OB of *Lady Luck* from the Carlton Theatre was satisfactory, because the stage was not too big and the set used happened to be one which helped to exclude echo. But the broadcast of *Oh, Kay!* from His Majesty's was an almost total disaster—the cast moved about the huge stage so freely that even five microphones proved insufficient to catch the dialogue and lyrics, and Gertrude Lawrence's big number *Someone to Watch Over Me* went almost for nothing on the air.

While struggling unsuccessfully against the ban, the BBC produced musical comedies of its own—some of them entirely successful. Eric Maschwitz, a former editor of *Radio Times* who had once also been a broadcaster especially responsible for church services, collaborated with George Posford to write *Good Night, Vienna*, broadcast in 1932; it was such a success that Herbert Wilcox bought the film rights, and it was produced as the first British musical talkie, with Anna Neagle and Jack Buchanan.

The late '20s and very early '30s were years in which the BBC was really establishing itself. The popularity of programmes—the vast popularity of dance music and variety programmes, and the increasing popularity of talks and more serious programmes—was making it evident that radio was

becoming an absolutely integral part of everyday life. By the end of 1931, the number of receiving licences in Great Britain and Northern Ireland had passed four million. Over 25,000 free licences had been issued to the blind—and many people listened then, as now, without a licence.

It may be that insufficient tribute has been paid to the role played by the announcers during radio's childhood years. Quite apart from being the best known voices in the country, they had a very real responsibility for the successful running of the Corporation. They were, in the early days, solely responsible for ensuring that the advertised programmes were broadcast to a proper timetable. Each day, the senior announcer would collect the following day's scripts and an up-to-date list of the day's programmes; last-minute 'news flashes' or SOS calls would, of course, have to be slipped in at the last moment. (The BBC broadcast SOS messages seeking the relatives of dangerously ill people if all other means to contact them had failed; requests for information about missing people would only be broadcast if New Scotland Yard or a Chief Constable requested it. In 1927, 1,549 SOSs were broadcast).

On the following morning, he would issue the material to the duty announcer, so that he could make himself thoroughly familiar with it before the day's broadcasting began. The senior

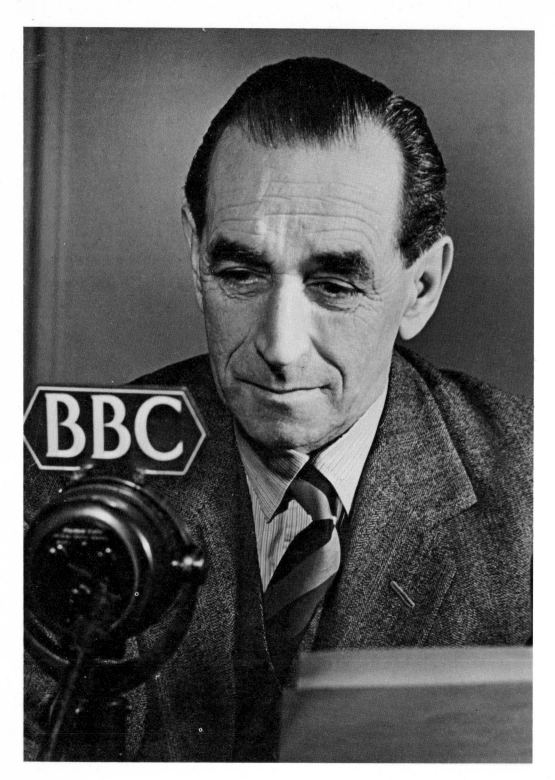

evening announcer would take over from the daytime announcer at 7 pm, and would take charge of the seven Savoy Hill studios and 'all matters in connection with the performance of the programmes'. There would be other announcers available, of course, for any additional work—but the senior announcer of the evening would announce all the important programmes, and read the second General News Bulletin. This—the 9 o' clock news, followed by the weather forecast—attracted more listeners than any other programme. Good time-keeping was of course essential, especially in view of the growing number of provincial broadcasting stations which would 'opt out' at various times for their own programmes. Announcers—and listeners—were, by 1928, helped by a number of official BBC time-checks: the Greenwich time-signal was broadcast compulsorily once a day by 2 LO (at 6.30 pm), and Big Ben once a day, at noon. There were other time-checks when possible, and announcers were responsible for getting programmes safely off the air in time for these. One pianist, Hershel Henlea, was famous for always overrunning her allotted time: announcers simply faded down her microphone, and she went on playing to herself in the studio, unaware that the world outside was by then listening to Jack Payne.

Auditions for announcers were tough, and the training tougher. Freddie Grisewood, before his appointment was confirmed in 1930, underwent a forty-five minute test at the microphone, with newsreading, readings of prose and poetry, an imaginary emergency with which he had to deal, the announcement of orchestral programmes with the names of foreign works and conductors to pronounce, sample texts in German, French and Italian, an unseen short story and—an intelligence test! A board of true BBC men, including senior announcers, chaired by A. Lloyd James, Secretary of the Advisory Committee, listened carefully behind locked doors.

Auditions for artistes were quite as frightening as those for staff, and certainly as fairly conducted. A panel of distinguished musicians, for instance, would listen to singers in a room some distance from the studio, judging solely by what they could hear over the loudspeaker. So fair were the auditions, indeed, that at one meeting the chairman glumly remarked: 'Well, gentlemen, you have just failed the daughter of the chairman of the Board of Governors!'

Announcers had to cope with the ordinary human propensity for error. Sometimes mistakes were not altogether their fault. One announcer innocently read out an announcement promising a performance of Holst's ballet music for *The Perfect Foot*—a secretary not knowing her 'l' from her 't'. Sometimes the

Freddie Grisewood, for many years a BBC announcer, found his greatest fame at the end of his career as the conductor of *Any Questions*

47

Stuart Hibberd, one of radio's most impressive and beloved voices during the '30s and '40s

programme planners put their feet in it: Stuart Hibberd found himself announcing a performance of three madrigals, in February 1928. They were, in order, *In Going to my Naked Bed, Fair Phyllis I Saw, To Shorten Winter's Sadness.*

Music took up a fair deal of the early announcers' time, for most of them sometimes sang—both Frank Phillips and Stuart Hibberd sang hymns during the *Epilogue*. And they were often required to turn over the music for visiting soloists. One musical ignoramus, turning the music 'on the nod' for a pianist, muffed it and dropped a page, quickly picked it up and re-placed it—upside down. One day in 1930, Hibberd, sitting in a continuity studio, was broadcasting some gramophone records. Carried away by a Beecham performance of Berlioz' *Hungarian March*, he sang along with it—and telephone calls to Savoy Hill soon revealed that a fault in a microphone connection was resulting in his voice being broadcast as well as the record.

Some announcers' mistakes are of course classic, my own favourite being that of the announcer reading a report of a smash-and-grab raid. The news script (news scripts are noto-riously not among the BBC's most literate contributions to broadcasting) stated firmly 'The thieves made their get-away in a fast car.' The announcer, justifiably, pressed down the 'cough key' enabling him to speak to the studio manager without being heard by listeners, and commented, 'You'd hardly expect them to use a slow one.' The key failed to work.

Similarly, Stuart Hibberd was listening one night to Sir Kingsley Wood, then Minister of Health, finishing a broadcast on pensions, when another announcer, Lionel Marson, discussing with the news editor items for the coming news broadcast, was offered an item about the womanising rector of Stiffkey. 'What, that bloody man again?', said Marson—just as Sir Kingsley ended his speech, and the microphone was opened for the closing announcement. The telephones were soon hot with incoming protests—as they were when Hibberd himself, a few years later, was irritated by a flickering red light, and without realising that his microphone was 'live', said nervously 'What the hell?'. In Paris the newspapers that evening printed the headline: *REVOLUTION A LA BBC*!

But as many an announcer's blunder has shown him, the public enjoys nothing so much as an honest—and, if possible, farcical—error.

It was Stuart Hibberd, probably the best loved announcer the BBC ever employed, who was responsible for inventing the 'Goodnight' for which he was famous: 'Goodnight everybody,' he would say, then pause for four counts before repeating 'Goodnight'. Hundreds of thousands of people all over the country bid him goodnight during the pause. Only the strict policy of anonymity prevented early BBC announcers having the best known names, as well as voices, in the land. Meanwhile, there was of course, a lot of speculation about their real personalities and private lives—speculation Eric Maschwitz satirised in a song written for a BBC party and sung by a BBC charwoman:

Do announcers make good husbands?
Do they gamble, drink or swear?
Or linger outside Selfridge's
Staring 'ard at underwear?
Oh, 'andsome is as 'andsome does, the proverb may be trite,
A man may be a wrong 'un, though 'is accent may be right,
If 'e leaves 'is teeth in Milton on the lino overnight . . .
Oh, are they the same at 'ome?

It should not be forgotten that the BBC was not having things entirely its own way on the radio waves. The use of the wireless for commercial gain was too tempting for business not

to have a crafty shot at a quick profit. In 1925, one Captain
L. F. Plugge approached Selfridge's to see if they would be
interested in paying for a talk on fashion to be delivered from
the Eiffel Tower broadcasting station in Paris. They were.
Three listeners wrote in to say that they had heard it. Three
years later, a firm making radios started a series of Sunday
evening concerts of light music from Radio Hilversum, when
de Groot's orchestra played for an hour after the BBC had
closed down. There were other broadcasts from Radio Toulouse
—and they were actually advertised in *Radio Times*!

Reith apparently took that kind of competition easily: it
only affected a tiny proportion of BBC listeners living within
the reception area. But, in 1929, things hotted up: business
firms began to advertise on Radio Paris, a powerful long-wave
station. A year later came Radio Luxembourg, then Radio
Normandie (with a larger potential audience in Britain than in
France). A firm of radio manufacturers started a Sunday-night
gramophone record programme, which, Reith noted disap-
provingly, was broadcast 'in a blatant American manner'.

Despite attempts to keep it off the air, then to *get* it off,
Radio Luxembourg was a great success, and for the first time
British listeners were heard whistling and singing the equivalent
of television commercial jingles. ('We are the Ovaltinies,/Little
girls and boys' is burned into a good few consciousnesses as
well as my own, I shouldn't wonder.) The International
Broadcasting Union attempted to put its foot down, but Radio
Luxembourg continued to be a success, closely followed by
Radio Normandie (the property of Captain Plugge, now a Tory
MP), and continued to broadcast until World War II.

It was in 1932 that the BBC left Savoy Hill. For some time
it had been obvious that the Corporation could not stay there
much longer. It could just about deal with that proportion of
the staff of 773 actually engaged in broadcasting in 1926 (though
the word 'cosy', often applied by elderly broadcasters to the
studios there must have been something of an understatement).
By 1931, when the staff had grown to almost 1,300, things were
getting desperate. So, on 14 May of the following year, Stuart
Hibbert described in his diary a programme entitled *The Last
of Savoy Hill*.

Towards the end of this programme a group of engineers,
having closed down the Savoy Hill control-room for the
last time, descended the steps leading to the main entrance,
talking to one another. They were followed a little later by
myself, and listeners could hear my conversation with
Oliver, the night watchman, as I sauntered slowly down the

familiar staircase, my mind full of memories. My appearance was Oliver's cue to remove the iron shutter and open the small door in it to let me out into the street. While this was going on, I paused and said to him: 'Well, Oliver, I suppose this is the last time you'll be pulling down that old shutter for me?'

'Yes, Sir,' he replied; 'this is the end of Savoy Hill.'

But a few minutes later, a strange voice ended that programme: a voice which marked the opening of a new epoch. 'This', it announced, 'This is Broadcasting House calling.'

III This is Broadcasting House

Broadcasting House might have stood in Trafalgar Square, Adelphi Terrace, Exhibition Road, or the Haymarket—sites in all those places were considered by the BBC during the 1920s. But, finally, the Corporation decided on Portland Place and a slightly eccentrically shaped site where Foley House had once stood—a house designed by James Wyatt (several fireplaces from which are in the Victoria and Albert Museum).

After a few difficulties had been overcome (an old brick conduit carrying a stream from the neighbourhood of Hampstead had to be enclosed, and a special means of minimising traffic vibration contrived), work went ahead on Colonel G. Val Myer's £350,000 building, which has so often been compared to a great ocean liner sailing down Portland Place towards Oxford Circus. In its foundations were buried a copy of the first issue of *Radio Times*, the first three issues of the *Handbook* (before it was retitled the *Yearbook*), and copies of the agreement to purchase the site.

At first, it was planned to place all the studios at the top of the building, as far away as possible from the traffic noise. But (fortunately, in view of the enormous noise increase to come over the next years) the shape of the site made this impossible, and in the end Colonel Myer decided to encase all the studios in a sort of tower at the centre of the building, where normally a light well might have been expected. A thick brick wall rose to surround the studios and outside it were the offices, with plenty of light. An elaborate air-conditioning system—in its time one of the best in the world—was devised for the studios, and they were divided from each other by book stores, libraries, and other rooms from which there would not be enough noise to disturb broadcasting.

The decoration of the building and studios was in the best of the taste of the time and, if it had been possible to preserve it complete—alas, only remnants survive here and there—the building would be a complete masterpiece of its age. Fortunately, various souvenir books published at the time of its completion preserve a record of how the various rooms looked— the talks studio, a fake library with wall-to-wall bookcases filled with book-backs gummed onto plaster; the religious studio for the broadcasting of services (which it was at first proposed to consecrate, until it was discovered that the consecration of a building involved the space between heaven and earth, so that it would have meant also consecrating several offices and part of the canteen kitchens); the vaudeville studio in the basement, with seventy-seven seats and a stage fitted with spotlights 'designed to give the performers a sufficient illusion of being in their more familiar environment of stage and footlights', and the main drama studio, with

a large tank for water noises; a wind machine; a railway noises group; various types of floor materials for floor effects; a compressed air group, including hooters and fog-horns; a small piano; a barrel organ; special doors for opening, shutting, slamming &c; suspended sheets for thunder; and drums of various sizes.

Broadcasting House, in Portland Place, was not very old when the coming of war necessitated the piling of sandbags on the pavements outside. The building was damaged by enemy action, but broadcasting never faltered

With its keen sense of involvement in the arts, it is not surprising that the BBC instructed its architect to provide space in the new building for some groups of sculpted figures. Eric Gill, whose carvings of the Stations of the Cross in Westminster Cathedral had been much admired, was commissioned to provide several pieces, the most elaborate being a group of Prospero and Ariel, to stand above the main entrance, looking down towards Regent Street.

Gill, with his keenly sensual appreciation of the human figure, carved a draped Prospero gently offering Ariel to the world. The boy, his pipes held over his head, was nude, and there is a strong tradition that Reith, when he first saw the figure, was somewhat disturbed by its extremely apparent maleness. Not wishing to make any critical comment based only on objective emotion (unlike the charwoman who, coming across the figure for the first time, was heard to remark to a friend: 'Cor, what a whopper he'll have when he grows up!'), Reith is said to have summoned the headmaster of a famous public school, who might be expected to be familiar with the average vital statistics of the young male figure. The headmaster regarded the carving for some time, turned to Reith, and said: 'Well, Sir John, I can fairly say that in my experience the young man does appear to be remarkably well hung.' The sculptor was thereupon instructed to reduce Ariel's genitalia to more modest proportions.

The BBC and its *Yearbook* were enormously proud of the new building, and rightly so; but the fact of the matter is that it was too small even before it was finished. Offices had to be subdivided, there was over-booking of studios, and it was soon necessary even to modify the decor because it got in the way of efficient working. Many of the broadcasters who moved from Savoy Hill found the new building cramped and unsatisfactory. Stuart Hibberd thought it depressing, with box-like studios and a 'low' atmosphere. On 7 July 1932, however, the King and Queen paid a visit, and the Wireless Singers welcomed them with a chorus of *I Want to be Happy* (substituted, at the last minute, for an Elizabethan madrigal).

To celebrate the start of broadcasting from the new studios, an extra two and a half hours of programmes were offered on Sunday, when broadcasting now started at midday (there was still a ninety-minute break in transmission at 6 pm, so that radio would not be in competition with the churches). At the first service broadcast from the religious studio, a blessing was asked on 'all who will speak, or sing, or play . . . that they may give of their best whether grave or gay, instructive or humorous . . .'.

54

By now, listeners had a real choice of programmes. Many of the protests received from members of the public (though there were always, in the early days, more letters of appreciation than of protest) were from people who didn't like chamber music and would rather be listening to *Music Hall*, or people who found *Grand Hotel* sentimental pap and would rather have a talk on Bartok. After 1930, there were two programmes to chose from: National and Regional—the first to be heard throughout Great Britain and Northern Ireland, and the second transmitted by the London Regional Station, parts of it being included in the programmes of the regions, which also originated their own programmes in contrast with those on the National Network.

The licence fee was still only ten shillings (50p)—of which 4s 7d went to the BBC and 5s 5d to the Government. Of its share, the BBC spent 2s 6½d on programmes; the rest went on engineering, rents, administration and Governors' salaries (one farthing).

The BBC still clung to mixed programme scheduling—a system which is remembered with affection by many listeners. It seems to have been Reith who, during his years as Director General, stood out against a radio channel entirely devoted to light entertainment (when one was later operated, it was known, inevitably, as 'the Light Programme'). Under Reith the BBC's assumption was that the intelligent listener should be able to enjoy any type of programme provided that it was sufficiently high in quality. Reith's 'ideal listener' should be able to pay attention during one evening to a classical music concert, a cinema-organ recital, the news, some poetry, a revue, an OB perhaps of some after-dinner speeches, and the *Epilogue*. The fact that this 'ideal listener' did not exist was, of course, perfectly well known to Reith, but this did not prevent him from postulating one, and attempting to ensure that he was well served. It was a noble ideal, and made British broadcasting the best in the world.

One of the fields in which radio was on the whole rather slow to get going, was drama. Though there had been drama productions of a kind in the very early days, even as late as 1930 plays only took up 1.49 per cent of the total broadcasting time on the National network as opposed, say, to dance music, which occupied 11.48 per cent of the time, talks and discussions (11.17 per cent) and *Children's Hour* (6.08 per cent). But in the 1930s there grew a realisation that radio drama could be extremely effective, and need by no means confine itself to adaptations of popular novels or stage plays. Indeed, in the *Yearbook* for 1931, it was recognised that a play specially

Though actors occasionally had to be held at the microphone to prevent them moving around the studio as if on stage, they did not dress in stage costumes for a broadcast. The cast of *Lady Precious Stream*, performed for the wireless in 1935, posed in costume for a publicity photograph. (*left to right*) Esme Percy, Mabel Constanduros, Carol Combe and Roger Livesey

written for radio by Ernst Johannson—*Brigade-Exchange*—had 'achieved a far greater effect than the very fine production of *Journey's End* on Armistice Day.'

The upward swing seems to have begun in 1930, for, apart from Johannson's play, there were productions of Shaw's *St Joan*, Compton Mackenzie's *Carnival* (adapted for radio in a two-hour version, and much acclaimed), *Twelfth Night* and three other Shakespeare plays, and adaptations of several novels including *Rupert of Hentzau*, *Lord Jim* and *Typhoon*.

It is no coincidence that the increased liveliness of radio drama was noticed just after the appointment of Val Gielgud as the BBC's Production Director, responsible for variety and drama, but most interested in drama. He encouraged Lance Sieveking to produce *The First Kaleidoscope*, and Tyrone Guthrie to write and produce *The Squirrel's Cage* and *The Flowers are not for You to Pick*, which were real landmarks in the history of radio drama. He even supervised the broadcasting of an uncut version of *Othello* with Henry Ainley, and persuaded Reith to accept the idea of a World Theatre series which started with the Gilbert Murray translation of Euripides' *Hippolytus*, with Godfrey Tearle, Diana Wynyard and Gladys

Young (to become perhaps the best loved radio actress of her time).

Of course, mistakes were made—producers were often unable to resist the temptation to play with the new toy of 'sound effects' (still described in BBC scripts as 'FX'), with the result that wind and waves were occasionally louder than the actors they were supposed to support; shots were heard in the sedate corridors outside the Director General's Office in Savoy Hill, as producers strove to melodramatise a mystery, and engineers were always experimenting with coconut shells and other pieces of bric-a-brac. Val Gielgud has described how, after a recording of seagulls especially made on the Thames embankment had been found to be of less than splendid quality, George Inns produced the sound of screaming gulls required for the end of *Carnival* with 'some elastic and a piece of wood'.

At Broadcasting House, with its new studios and effects machines, things were technically a little less strained, and while producers sometimes moaned that production was 'less fun' than in the old improvisatory days, the listeners undoubtedly gained.

By now, theatre managements had realised that radio brought

It was often difficult for the BBC to get permission to broadcast the West End productions of plays or musicals; occasionally, they produced their own versions. Here, after a rehearsal of Noël Coward's *Bitter-Sweet*, are Betty Huntley-Wright, Eric Maschwitz, Evelyn Laye—who had played in the operetta in New York— a young Stanford Robinson, and Serge Abranovie

additional fame to stage performers and were only too happy for the BBC to broadcast plays which had been successful in the theatre. Dorothy Dickson played in a studio production of Edgar Wallace's *The Ringer*, Henry Ainley and Leon Quartermaine in Flecker's *Hassan*, Emlyn Williams in *Will Shakespeare* and Jeanne de Casalis (later a well known radio comédienne) with Harcourt Williams in *The Seagull*.

Chekov was safe enough, perhaps; other classics presented problems. When Gielgud conceived the idea of a radio production of Ibsen's *Ghosts*, for instance, he felt he should play it safe by getting permission, if not a blessing, from authority. The Deputy Director General, Admiral Carpendale, having read Clement Scott's famous description of the play as 'an open drain . . . a dirty act done publicly', took the script away, and returned it to the anxious Gielgud with the words: 'I don't see why you should want to do the thing. It's very long—and *very* dull.' So the production went ahead.

It was in 1937 that the Drama Department broadcast the first British 'soap opera'—*The English Family Robinson*, with that splendid character-actress Mabel Constanduros (whose Grandma Buggins was to become famous)—at the opposite end of a spectrum which also saw, in that same year, a production of Archibald McLeish's verse-play *The Fall of the City* in a new series entitled *Experimental Hour*. Both of these conceptions—the soap opera and *Experimental Hour*—were copied from American broadcasting. The first, alas, has continued with rather more popular success than the latter, and Val Gielgud made a bitter apology to the public in one of his autobiographies for having been responsible for blazing a trail which was to lead to *The Archers* and *The Dales* and *Waggoners' Walk*.

He might perhaps have been less apologetic: the serials have given an enormous amount of pleasure over the years and, however vapid, at their best initiated enormous popular interest—so much so that the BBC, whether calculatingly or not, managed to commandeer all the newspaper front pages on the day after the opening of commercial television by the simple device of immolating Grace Archer in a barn fire. But that day was still far away when the Robinsons were young.

An early glory of radio which was not, alas, to live on into the 1970s as the Drama Department does, was the establishment of the Features Department—for which Lance Sieveking was responsible. Towards the end of the Savoy Hill years, he established a group of producers to be responsible for 'general productions'. Originally, it was called the Research Section; later, it was to become Features, to attract radio producers and

(*far left*)
Robert Mawdesley as Walter
Gabriel with Eddie Robinson
as Simon Cooper, posing in
real farmyard muck during
the years when *The Archers*
was at the peak of its
popularity, with over eight
million listeners

'The incomparable Max'—
Max Beerbohm, between
1935 and 1945, made rare
but discriminating visits to
Broadcasting House. His
Sunday evening talks—
which included *Music Halls
of my Youth* and *London
Revisited*—had a pith and
elegance which made them
classics of radio

writers of such accomplishment as D. G. Bridson, Jack Dillon, Maurice Browne, Stephen Potter and Louis MacNeice, and to reach its apogee under the leadership of Laurence Gilliam, whose premature retirement (and the disbanding of Features) in 1964 remains one of the very few thoroughly foolish and disreputable acts the BBC establishment has committed. Its effects in demoralising those who worked in and for radio remain incalculable.

The range of Features in the early days was immediately very considerable: there were programmes about single men and their reputations (*Erasmus* and *Coleridge*); productions of great imaginative literary works, such as Gielgud's production of G. K. Chesterton's *Lepanto*, later re-produced for NBC in New York; commemorations of great occasions (*Waterloo* and *Gallipoli*); and 'straight' documentaries such as *The First or Grenadier Guards*, scripted by Sir Arthur Bryant. By the time the latter programme was produced, the BBC's reputation was such that, at a time when England was feverishly preparing for World War II, the Commanding Officer of the Regiment met Gielgud to discuss at length the number of paces marched to the minute by the Guards at Fontenoy.

The broadcast talk—which apart from occasional exceptions has perished with so many other good manifestations of early radio—was also extremely successful and popular during the 1930s. Once more, Reith was thoroughly behind it; one of the major aims of the BBC was to inform—and a good talk (really a literary essay in terms of radio) could entertain as well as inform —forty years on, Alistair Cooke's *Letter from America* continues to prove the point.

There were some splendid early 'talkers' broadcasting from Savoy Hill and Broadcasting House, led—socially, at all events —by His Majesty King George V. The King was a good and remarkably natural broadcaster. He had first broadcast in 1924, and not only addressed the microphone as a friend, but realised perfectly the extent to which it could be used to spread ideas. Regularly every year from 1932 until his death in 1935, he broadcast on Christmas Day at the end of Laurence Gilliam's Commonwealth programme.

'This is the King speaking to *you*', he would say—or once, in a special broadcast to children, 'Remember, children, the King is speaking to *you*.' Probably these broadcasts made him the best known King in English history up to that time, and no doubt they contributed to the popular burst of affection at the time of his Jubilee. On the eve of his death in 1935, the BBC took leave of him in an affecting way, cancelling all programmes from mid-evening onward, and simply repeating every fifteen minutes a message read by Stuart Hibberd: '*The King's life is moving peacefully towards its close.*' The effect of the broadcast was such that few people who heard it then do not, even now, speak of it as one of the most moving pieces of radio they ever encountered.

Among the King's fellow-broadcasters of 'talks' were Harold Nicolson, politician and man of letters, Vernon Bartlett, the BBC's foreign correspondent, Ernest Newman, the music critic, Max Beerbohm, the Edwardian essayist and John Hilton. Hilton was to become one of the most familiar broadcasters of his time, with an enormous range of interests, each of which he seemed able to make interesting for his listeners. He was a man of deep sympathies, and his broadcasts on the subject of unemployment and other social evils were remarkable for their understanding and persuasiveness.

But of course there were protests about John Hilton too—wasting time talking about the unemployed, for goodness sake! Even Lord Beveridge, who gave a series of six talks on the same subject in 1931, was attacked on the grounds that his natural sympathy for the underdog concealed a left-wing bias. Meanwhile, the Left was attacking the Corporation for not going far enough to explain to general listeners the poverty and worklessness which was making so many of their fellow-citizens miserable. And Lord Hailsham (the present peer's father) was condemning the BBC as 'a disruptive influence', while Sir Waldron Smithers asked the Postmaster General whether nothing could be done to force the BBC to stop using its monopoly for the promotion of socialist propaganda.

Reith believed that controversy—if genuine, and the result of the widest possible transmission of the greatest possible range of views—was a good thing, and in the end triumphed over his opponents, who (in the words of the *Morning Post*) were of the opinion that 'the average man and woman, when at leisure with the world, has not the slightest desire to be plunged into disputes' about politics, religion and industry.

One of the things the BBC's detractors forgot was that more of the British people were now capable of joining rational argument about current affairs than ever before, simply because of the information brought to them by radio. That information was not (and is not) nearly as comprehensive as that contained in a serious newspaper, but it was a great deal better than nothing.

It seems to have become true that many of the news and current affairs programmes on radio in the 1970s exist in the main to offer comment, sometimes informed and sometimes not, rather than hard news—partly, of course, because there is not enough hard news to fill the enormous amount of time now allotted to news broadcasting. In the 1930s, news still meant *news:* at first, it must be admitted, simply because the Corporation had to rely on Reuters, the Press Association, the Exchange Telegraph and Central News—the big agencies. Very gradually, it began to spread itself; news talks were born (Vernon Bartlett's *The Way of the World* was a pioneer programme), and in 1933 there was the first example of the news magazine—a late-night forty-five minute news bulletin which included live broadcasts from the Continent, an account of the opening of Liverpool Airport and, for the first time, a recording of an event which had occurred earlier in the day—a cup-tie from Wimbledon.

It was in 1934 that News gained its independence, and became a separate department. The coming of portable recording machines gave it new impact: the Blattner steel-tape recording technique (the tape had to be 'edited' with steel clippers and welded together; the joins went through the machine with a noise like that of a train negotiating points) enabled producers to use recorded material of news interest—though the nine-minute, twelve-inch record was more usually used. Incidentally, it was at about this time that the BBC Recorded Programmes Library—the sound archives—was set up, then containing 25,000 records, and today about 100,000, many of them of course long-playing, and preserving the voices of many famous people and events, from Tennyson and Gladstone to the present day.

It was also at this time that Richard Dimbleby joined the BBC. A 22-year-old editor of *Advertiser's Weekly*, he recorded his first piece (a description of a model engineering exhibition at the Royal Agricultural Hall) in May 1936, and made such an impression on Reith, it is said, that the latter telephoned the producer especially to state that he never wished to hear that young man's voice again.

Dimbleby's merits, however, outweighed the at first leaden quality of his prose; indeed, by dint of sheer application, he soon became easily the best ad-lib broadcaster in the business, able to describe scenes and events vividly without a single note. He had, too, a Fleet-Street-man's nose for news and the determination to be first with it. For the first time, radio news actually got 'scoops', and its reporters began agitating for more and better equipment, so that 'on-the-spot' descriptions could be broadcast. Any broadcaster will have had experience of engineers who insist that quality should come before anything else: but in 1937, when Dimbleby, through a fluke, broadcast an account of the burning-down of the Crystal Palace by linking his microphone to a public telephone booth, even the engineers realised that quality came second to actuality.

A broadcast from the Spanish/French border during the Spanish Civil War, in which Dimbleby described the terrible retreat of the demolished Republican Army, made it clear to everyone who heard it that he was the first thoroughly accomplished BBC news reporter. His reputation, despite disreputable treatment by the Corporation immediately after the war, was to grow steadily until, at the time of his death, he was to millions of listeners and viewers the absolute personification of all the Corporation stood for.

By now, outside broadcasts were in general much more successful: they were tested to the utmost in 1937, at the time of the Coronation, described in great detail for radio listeners (permission to broadcast it on the then very young television service had been refused). The Coronation provided the opportunity for one of the best remembered goofs ever to be made on radio: the notorious broadcast by Tommy Woodruffe describing the illumination of the fleet, off Spithead.

Woodruffe was a good and practised reporter, with a lively style. An ex-Lieutenant Commander, RN, he took to the newly invented 'lip-mike' (a miniature microphone which enabled a commentary to go on without being disturbed by extraneous noises) like a duck to water, and his commentaries on horseraces were fast, accurate and extremely graphic.

After a splendid broadcast on Coronation Day itself, when he described the scene from the top of Constitution Hill, he made his way down to Portsmouth in preparation for his broadcast from Spithead. Unfortunately (though he was no doubt delighted at the time) he was assigned to HMS *Nelson*, on which he had once served. He had an extremely good evening with some of his old friends, and by the time he made his way to his commentary position was as relaxed as a newt.

Back at Broadcasting House, Lionel Marson introduced him: 'This is the BBC Regional Service. The illumination of the fleet. We now take you over to HMS *Nelson*, for a commentary by Lieutenant Commander Thomas Woodruffe.'

There was then a long silence before, punctuated by heavy breathing and the sound of furniture being knocked about, Woodruffe began his commentary.

'At the present moment,' he said, 'the whole fleet's liddup—an' whenisay liddup, I mean liddup by fairy lamps—We've forgodden the whole Royal Review—we've forgodden-theroyreview—the whole thing's liddup by fa'ylamps . . .'.

Apparently paralysed with horror, no-one stopped him,

no-one even turned him off—at least not for three or four minutes. But eventually, Harman Grisewood, on duty in London, faded him out with an apology for 'bad technical quality.'

Sir John Reith, in his train next day, held in trembling hands a newspaper with the headline THE FLEET'S LID UP. But with great humanity, he only suspended Woodruffe for six weeks, and he returned to sports commentating with all his old *élan* (in the following year promising to eat his hat if Preston North End was beaten in its cup final game with Huddersfield, and beginning to do so as the final whistle blew). Meanwhile, listeners all over the country rang up the BBC to ask for the recording to be re-broadcast (no such luck: even today it is rarely heard), and Jack Hylton named his new review *The Fleet's Lit Up*. It ran for a very long time.

However successful news broadcasts, talks and outside broadcasts—even of sports events—might be, listener research made it quite clear that most people regarded radio as a medium of popular entertainment, and in 1933, pushed a little by the growing number of listeners turning for such entertainment to Radios Luxembourg, Toulouse and Fécamp, Reith sent for the Editor of *Radio Times*, Eric Maschwitz, and made him head of a new department—Variety.

Though they had formerly been under the wing of the Revue and Vaudeville Section, headed by Val Gielgud (who had no real interest in variety), several radio stars had managed to make their mark. Tommy Handley was already well known by the end of the 1920s; Leonard Henry specialised in making quick jokes on any subject offered by a member of the audience (the tradition is carried on in the 1970s—*Does the Team Think*); Stainless Stephen (like the others, trained in the musichall) was years ahead of Victor Borge in making punctuation audible: he simply verbalised it—'My sister has a boarding house full stop All the windows have stained glass dash Stained with the soup her boarders have thrown at them exclamation mark'.

When Maschwitz took over Variety, he inherited three extremely popular series: *Music Hall*, *The Kentucky Minstrels* (produced by Harry S. Pepper) and *Songs from the Shows*. He also took over seven producers, Stanford Robinson as Musical Director, and Henry Hall and the BBC Dance Orchestra. While he set up many new programmes, he also took a keen interest in the old ones, engaging many new performers for *Music Hall*—among them Vic Oliver and Sandy Powell.

In 1933, he conceived the idea of *In Town Tonight*, which was to run for over twenty years, with its famous introduction montage of the Piccadilly flowerseller's voice, the roar of

London's traffic, Eric Coates' *Knightsbridge March*, and the voice of Freddie Grisewood shouting 'Stop!'—at which point the traffic noise abruptly ceased, and the programme brought to listeners *'some of the interesting people who are In Town Tonight'*.

Maschwitz went to America several times before the war, paid considerable attention to the development of radio there, and brought several American comedians and singers to London. But his own taste lay much more in the world of romance, and he revived for radio many popular musical comedies—*The Lilac Domino, Bitter Sweet, The Geisha, The Student Prince* and *The Vagabond King* (in which the leading role was played by Bebe Daniels, later to become so popular in the radio show *Hi, Gang!*).

Scrapbook was another programme which was a product of the 1930s. It was first broadcast—compiled by Leslie Baily and Charles Brewer—in 1933, as *Scrapbook for 1913*, and immediately became enormously popular, providing, incidentally, many of the earliest recordings in the BBC's sound archives. Then there was *Monday Night at Seven*, which later became *Monday Night at Eight*. It had almost everything:

'Uncle Mac'—Derek McCulloch—was known to generations of children for his work in *Children's Hour*. Here, he visits a farm for the programme, and interviews a junior Larry the Lamb

comedy, music, detection (Inspector Hornleigh investigated) and Puzzle Corner, devised by Ronnie Waldman—and it had a very high listening figure. But there was a year still to wait for the great variety shows—for the procession from *Band-wagon* and *ITMA* to *Hello Cheeky* and *I'm Sorry, I'll Read that Again*—to begin.

A programme that continued to build its reputation during the 1930s was *Children's Hour*, which had from the very beginning preoccupied so many people in Broadcasting House. By the 1930s, the BBC had decided that it was really rather demeaning to sedate ladies and gentlemen to ask them to address each other as 'uncle' and 'auntie', and that practice was discontinued. (Though it is no doubt a fact that hundreds of thousands of middle-aged men and women still think of Derek McCulloch with gratitude and pleasure as 'Uncle Mac').

There was originally a Wireless Circle for the kiddies, and the Birmingham station soon had 10,000 members. 'Uncles' and 'aunties' received them personally, from time to time, at public parties—it is recorded that an Uncle Edgar once kissed 800 Birmingham children in an hour; some kind of record, one would think. 'Uncles' and 'aunties' also read birthday greetings for birthday children (local commercial television stations still do the same thing today), and sometimes a radio 'uncle' would guide one particular child to a hidden surprise present.

At first, it was all really a giant romp, which one suspects the 'uncles' and 'aunties' enjoyed as much as the children. A sense of higher purpose crept in, however, no doubt from the general influence of the Director General, whose idea of *Children's Hour* was 'clean, wholesome humour, some light music, and a thorough sprinkling of information attractively conveyed.' Well, why not? But if one could magically pick up a 1933 *Children's Hour* on a 1977 tranny, one would no doubt think it all extremely stuffy, with producers taking their line from the tenets of the Guides and Scouts movements, and providing a sort of audible version of *The Children's Newspaper*.

The richness of *Children's Hour*, despite (and to some extent because of) this attitude, is something no child growing up today can imagine. The sheer joy of *Toytown*, for instance, written by S. Hulme Beaman, has never been equalled by anything children's television has so far offered. Beaman was a mild man, a book illustrator, who every now and then would sidle into Broadcasting House with a new story involving some of the 400 inhabitants of Toytown. After his death in 1932, the thirty-six stories he had left were broadcast again and again, and the voices of Ralph de Rohan as Mr Grouser, Felix

Felton as the Mayor, Norman Shelley as Captain Brass, and Derek McCulloch as Larry the Lamb will go with many of us to our graves.

It was Norman Shelley who played Pooh, A. A. Milne's hero; it was only with the greatest difficulty that, recording a programme with him a few years ago, I was able to address him by his human name. He had created Pooh, he has said, by close study of E. H. Shepherd's drawings of that tubby philosopher, with his stiff arms and waddling walk. It was a masterpiece of radio acting.

Then there was Romany—the Rev Bramwell Evans, who took two children and a dog for imaginary walks through the English countryside, describing the wild life around him so naturally and vividly that his broadcasts brought one alive for the first time (even if one had grown up in the country) to the beauty and fascination of nature. Rag, Romany's spaniel, was the nominal father of hundreds of less distinguished Rags all over the country. Evans was a remarkable broadcaster, quite unconscious of the microphone—many of his talks were largely improvised, and the effects man had to be ready to provide countryside sounds on a verbal cue and at the drop of a walking stick.

Then . . . well, so many more: Norman and Henry Bones, the boy detectives; the Zoo Man, David Seth-Smith; the gardener, C. H. Middleton; the Worzel Gummidge stories, and the many, many dramatised classics. The slaughter of *Children's Hour* may have seemed inevitable to the BBC planners, but it is something difficult to forgive. An attempt was made to woo children back to radio in the 1970s, with a short-lived Saturday afternoon programme; but the gap had been too considerable, the habit of listening broken. That it is possible to interest children in radio was proved by the late David Munrow in his splendid series *Pied Piper*, in the good old tradition of educational musical programmes.

A habit which had never been broken was that of listening to music, however; and radio had always realised that music was one of its strongest suits. Dance music, certainly, but also 'serious' or 'classical' music. If the BBC has been responsible for nothing else in its long life, the popularisation of classical music, making England one of the most musical countries in the world, providing knowledgeable audiences for concerts and for opera, which are deeply appreciated by visiting musicians, would mark it down for gratitude by anyone to whom the arts are of the least importance.

Two men led the BBC's musical planning during the late 1920s and '30s—Percy Pitt and Sir Adrian Boult. Mr Pitt laid

the foundations of the BBC's policy during his time as Music Adviser and, later, Director of Music (1923–29). He arranged for the broadcasting of the classics, but also of work by contemporary composers such as Bartok and Hindemith (who played their own work), Alan Bush and Stravinsky. He arranged for the broadcasting of over twenty symphony concerts within one year, during several of which Beecham conducted the music of Frederick Delius (there is a marvellous portrait of Delius listening to one of those concerts).

Adrian Boult took over from him in 1929, and as a brilliant conductor made the BBC Symphony Orchestra one of the best in the world (as Toscanini told him after conducting it in the late 1930s). It is heart-warming that his association has continued; as I write he is still conducting at the Promenade Concerts, giving magnificent performances of Elgar.

One of the BBC's major achievements was the 'saving' of Sir Henry Wood's Promenade Concerts. Wood had conducted the first Prom in 1895—it had a programme that would astonish and amuse an audience at the Albert Hall today: Wagner's overture *Rienzi* jostled Kennington's *Thou Hast Come*, and Liszt's *Hungarian Rhapsody* was not far distant from Schubert's *Serenade*, played upon the trumpet by Mr Howard Reynolds!

The Proms had been founded by Wood in collaboration with Robert Newman; and when Newman died, it was generally thought that the Queen's Hall would no longer see the annual repetition of the popular series. Then Reith personally managed to sign a contract with William Boosey, the manager of the Hall (and for years as determined an opponent of broadcasting as Sir Oswald Stoll), and it was announced that the 1927 Proms would be broadcast, with 'Sir Henry Wood and his Symphony Orchestra'.

Wood was delighted. He had for years been forced to subdue his natural inclinations and include in his programmes music which he did not consider to be of a reputable standard, but which would bring in the paying customers. Now, he realised, he was free from the problem which faces almost every concert promoter, and dogs the concert halls: the conflict between a good programme, and a good ticket-selling programme.

'I felt really elated', he wrote of the first BBC Prom, 'I realised that the work of such a large part of my life had been saved from an untimely death. I do not think I ever conducted Elgar's joyous *Cockaigne* overture with greater spirit than on this occasion.'

The BBC's support meant things other than freedom to

Sir Henry Wood broadcast for the first time in 1927; but it was the 'Proms'—his conception, but only possible through the BBC's support—which made him a still more famous national figure

Sir Adrian Boult, sometime
musical director of the BBC,
and between 1941 and 1950
its Conductor in Chief. A
generous and revered
musician

build proper programmes: it meant regular daily rehearsals, and plenty of time to search for new works and prepare unfamiliar ones. Wood, a great musician and sometimes also a great conductor, gave the first performance of Mahler's *Symphony of a Thousand* at a broadcast Prom (in 1930); with the relatively new BBC Chorus, he gave Elgar's *Dream of Gerontius* on Good Friday 1938; he broadcast Wagner's *Parsifal* complete at a time when staging of the opera in England was extremely rare. A few recordings of the period show just how good some of the performances were—and the orchestra had some marvellous players, among them Paul Beard, the leader, Aubrey Brain (horn) and Archie Camden (bassoon).

There is a general idea that Wood was a conductor chary of presenting new music. The opposite is the truth: among the 'novelties' he conducted at the Proms between 1927 and 1937 were Walton's *Portsmouth Point* and *Viola Concerto*, Kodály's *Hary Janos*, Sibelius' *Tapiola*, Strauss' *Symphonia Domestica*, E. J. Moeran's *Rhapsody No 2*, Ireland's *Piano Concerto*, Webern's *Passacaglia*, Bartok's *Hungarian Peasant Songs*, Bliss' music for the film *Things to Come*, Shostakovitch's *First Symphony* and *First Piano Concerto*, and Rubbra's *Violin Fantasia*.

Wood also conducted other concerts, including a series 'at Woolworth's prices' from the People's Palace in the Mile End Road, where Beecham and Elgar also conducted. Beecham had at first thought little of broadcasting. Listening in the days when microphones were rudimentary, and incapable of reproducing properly the sounds of the individual instruments, he had found broadcast music 'the most abominable row that ever stunned and cursed the human ear'. Long negotiations with him over the foundation of a new orchestra to be sponsored by the Corporation eventually came to nothing; but when the BBC Symphony Orchestra was formed in 1930, he was forced to admit that it contained the best instrumentalists in the country.

Boult was in fine fettle, threw himself with gusto into training the orchestra, and its first appearance at the Queen's Hall in October was a triumph—a triumph repeated on tours to Brussels, Paris, Zürich, Vienna and Budapest. One of its problems was space for rehearsal and performance: it really needed its own studio. At first it rehearsed and played in an old warehouse on the site of the present National Theatre, fitted out as a studio, and in 1934 moved to a studio converted from a skating rink in Maida Vale, where it still regularly plays.

Opera had always been broadcast, but again there were difficulties in the way of regular performances. The International Grand Opera season at Covent Garden allowed three acts of opera a fortnight to be broadcast, in return for the loan of Percy Pitt to conduct the season (not perhaps a very generous bargain for the BBC). Some artistes would not allow themselves to be broadcast at all—Florence Austral, for instance, was one of these—and there were often natural hazards like Sir Thomas Beecham to be dealt with. He once made a long speech on the air rebuking the BBC for keeping the theatre audience waiting while some announcer read a synopsis of the opera.

Soon, however, the BBC's patronage was recognised as well worth having. Reith managed to negotiate a state grant for the Covent Garden Opera Syndicate in 1930—which predictably attracted the attention of the *Daily Express* ('There are better ways of spending £17,500 than in subsidising a form of art which is not characteristic of the British people'!) During the 1930s the BBC gave a lot of financial help not only to Covent Garden, but to the Carl Rosa touring company, and to Sadler's Wells; and it broadcast opera from Glyndebourne as early as 1935. Opera broadcasts were quite as frequent as they are today: in 1932, the BBC broadcast thirteen full-length operas from Covent Garden, thirteen from the Wells and the Old Vic, and a number from the provinces.

Then there were studio performances: without the necessity to provide scenery and costumes, the BBC could afford to revive less popular and well known works—Boult was particularly eager to do this. Massenet's *Manon* was the first opera to be produced in the studio during Boult's time (in 1939), and Vaughan Williams' *Hugh the Drover* was given in the same year.

All this was building up an enormous audience for music in Great Britain—and in the coming years its manifestation at the Proms was to be to a large degree the wonder of the world: there is still nothing anywhere quite like the Promenade Concerts, with their ebullient first and last nights, with all the highspirited frippery, the ludicrous magnificence of the singing of long out-dated patriotic songs, and the devout attention to great music which makes the Prom audiences unique.

Henry Wood and Adrian Boult were to a large degree responsible for all this: but so was Reith. He took a deep personal interest in the broadcasting of music—but then, he took a deep personal interest in all broadcasting and all broadcasters. The more one considers this astonishing man, the more remarkable he appears: a man who had an iron control and built the BBC largely in his own image; who could command immediate obedience and loyalty, yet on the whole failed to command affection; a man who could take a panoramic view—yet could dismiss an announcer who was about to figure as the *innocent* party in a divorce case, or could forgive another caught in an unwonted embrace with his secretary, but with the reservation that he should never again be allowed to read the *Epilogue*!

Reith did not suffer fools gladly, and believed that there were several of them about. 'You can't think rationally on an empty stomach, and a whole lot of people can't do it on a full stomach either,' he once remarked. He had little sympathy with 'new thinking' of any kind. He seems to have liked to be surrounded by 'yes-men'. He took a hand in—'interfered with' is the phrase some of his employees used—programmes he thought needed his substantial and moral touch. He personally travelled to Windsor to introduce the voice of King Edward VIII when the latter made his abdication speech—having disobeyed the Prime Minister's instruction that no broadcasting link with the Castle should be organised. He had no patience with those who took opposite views to his own. Questioned by Malcolm Muggeridge for television after World War II, the most he would concede to differences of opinion was the splendidly equivocal Scots phrase 'I hear you'—meaning just that; neither agreement nor disagreement being implied.

Yet one would choose, with hindsight, no-one but Reith to have started the BBC. He stood out implacably against the yowling and twitching of politicians, businessmen, and the Press on both left and right. He defended the independence of broadcasters up to the hilt. He fought for and won the BBC's right to express opinions on current affairs, despite frenetic opposition. He dominated Savoy Hill and Broadcasting House as an Everest would dominate the Gog Magog Hills. Whatever his faults, he was a great man.

One of his ambitions in life was to be 'fully stretched', to feel that he was straining every intellectual muscle, using every part of himself completely. He would have had no word for Browning's phrase about one's reach exceeding one's grasp. And at the BBC, he felt, astonishingly, that he was in a lesser position than he could and should command. Indeed, he was always to feel this; perhaps only the Prime Ministership, or, more properly, the dictatorship, of England would have given him the sensation he sought (and what a disaster that would have been for the country!) In 1938, he decided to retire. The thought had crossed his mind even earlier; now, he instrumented it. In June, he told the Board of Governors that he intended to accept an offer to become chairman of Imperial Airways.

Crassly, the Governors did not invite him to be present at the discussions to fix on a successor. Mortally offended, Reith let it be known that he did not wish to be offered a seat on the Board, gave orders for his BBC radio and TV sets to be returned from his home to Broadcasting House, and without any ceremony one day simply took the lift from his third-floor office to the entrance of Broadcasting House, and, tears rolling down his face, let the heavy doors swing shut behind him.

That evening he drove out to Droitwich for dinner with some old friends, and that night himself switched off the transmitter after programmes had closed down. He was invited to sign the visitors' book. He wrote:

J. C. W. Reith—late BBC.

IV Home and Forces

In 1937, the BBC planned a new sort of variety show. Really large audiences, it had been discovered, were attracted to variety more than almost anything else. Listener-research had shown, by 1936, that while over three quarters of all listeners spent one-sixth of their time listening to the dance-band programmes, one half listened to *all* studio variety programmes, and broadcasts from variety theatres were by far the favourite programmes. *Music Hall* attracted 61 per cent of all listeners.

It was also noticed that variety programmes from overseas stations—Luxembourg and Normandie especially—occasionally attracted up to 80 per cent of the home audience at times when the BBC was only offering a talk or an educational programme. Obviously there was an enormous regular audience to be captured, and Eric Maschwitz was out to capture it. He went around the variety theatres to hear new comics, he talked to writers and producers, and eventually he made appointments to meet two comedians he thought might take the centre of a new show. He arranged to meet them at two pubs near Broadcasting House. He never got to the second pub—for in the first was Arthur Askey.

Askey was making his living at the time as a comic touring the halls and appearing a great deal at 'masonics'—evening entertainments arranged by Freemasons or similar organisations. In 1936, he compèred a radio variety show called *February Fill-Dyke*, which had not been a glorious success; but Maschwitz thought that the eager little man with the chirpy style had possibilities. With Askey, he teamed a rather different personality—Richard Murdoch, a light comedian who had previously worked in revue. They were to be involved in a new adventure each week, in a show to be called *Bandwagon*.

Arthur Askey and Richard ('Stinker') Murdoch

Arthur's Inn, a weekly comedy series in which Arthur plays the part of the proprietor of an almost poverty-stricken inn. Brian Reece amends the script while (*left to right*) Sally Ann Howes, Arthur Askey and Diana Decker seem to disagree

Like every successful show, *Bandwagon* took its time to get going. Though it had been planned to run for thirteen weeks (the statutory quarter-year for which most series are planned), there was some talk of taking it off after only five or six. Then, quite suddenly, in the inexplicable way in which such things happen, it caught the public's imagination, and piles of letters began to make their way to Broadcasting House and the imaginary flat on the top floor allegedly occupied by Arthur and 'Stinker' as official custodians of the Greenwich time-signal pips.

The show's signature-tune marked, every Wednesday evening, a half-hour during which the great majority of listeners tuned in to hear the weekly adventures of Arthur, 'Stinker', Lewis the goat and the impregnable Nausea Bagwash, their landlady's daughter—adventures which inevitably ended with Arthur involved in some fearful physical calamity, necessitating the kicking-over of a huge pile of tins in the studio, making the din with which the half-hour always ended.

The show moved very fast. Its script was carefully planned
and written to keep situations on the move, to provide a liberal
spicing of gags and catch-phrases: '*You silly little man!*'
'*Proper humdrum!*' and, most famous of all, Arthur's inimitable
'*I theng-you!*' There were four bright musical interludes
provided by Jack Hylton and his band; there was 'Chestnut
Corner', in which dreadful old jokes were welcomed by the
sound of a whistle or a rattle . . . and there was 'Mr Walker
Wants to Know', in which the delightful old Cockney comedian
Syd Walker told an anecdote, described a situation or a problem, and ended up: '*What would you do, chum?*' It was another
irresistible catch-phrase, and brought thousands of postcards
from listeners ready to tell him *just* what they would have done.

Bandwagon was far and away the most successful light-
entertainment show broadcast until that time. Its style was new,
it was inventive and witty; it made stars of Askey and Murdoch
overnight. By the time the show was drawing to the end of its
run, Askey could ask £600 a week for theatre performances,

which was just as well, because the fees the BBC paid him were negligible. Not unnaturally, Maschwitz decided he was on to a good thing, which had better be followed up. This time, perhaps a show could be built around a comedian already quite well known on radio—Tommy Handley?

Handley had 'gone on the stage'—his ambition since he was a young child—when he was twenty-three, and found himself in the Army during World War I. As a light baritone, he took part in over a thousand shows before being demobbed and joining the cast of a touring version of *Shanghai*, an undistinguished musical comedy. For the next year or so, he was undecided which way to turn, and it was more or less by accident that he discovered the script of a sketch about an Army court martial, set to the music of popular songs of the day. He adopted *The Disorderly Room* as his own, and used it for the next twenty years. He was asked to perform it in the Royal Command Variety Performance of 1924—and that performance was broadcast.

A little while afterwards, he was asked to do an audition for the BBC, and though he forgot his lines and thought he had made a thorough mess of the whole thing, it was a successful

'Can I do yer now, Sir?' Broadcasts of *ITMA* came to a stop for some time when the best-known characters said their opening lines. One of the most popular was Mrs Mopp, played by Dorothy Summers (*left*). With her and Tommy Handley is Jean Capra, as Poppy-Poo-Pah (1944)

audition. For the next fifteen years he worked for radio on and off, appearing in *Children's Hour*, *The White Coons' Concert Party*, and other shows, while making most of his living from stage appearances and films.

Francis Worsley, a BBC producer, decided in 1939 that it might be possible to build a fast-talking show around Handley, rather like the new American cross-talk shows which were such a success across the Atlantic. He commissioned several scripts from various writers, none of which seemed to work very well; and then one day he met with Handley and a new writer, Ted Kavanagh, in a room in the Langham Hotel in Portland Place. The Langham, once an extremely handsome and fashionable hotel, has played an important part in radio history—it is now entirely occupied by the BBC, with a reference library set in the handsome pillared Palm Court, and a bar and refreshment room in what was once the restaurant.

Sitting in the corner of a room crowded with clergymen who had come to the Langham for some ecclesiastical conference or other, Worsley, Kavanagh and Handley devised a programme set on an ocean cruise ship, with the comedian accompanied by a silly secretary (to be played by Celia Eddy, who

A first read-through of an *ITMA* script, written as usual by Ted Kavanagh (*right*). From left to right, the actors are Dorothy Summers, Jack Train, Tommy Handley and Paula Green

Tommy Handley became
probably the most instantly
recognisable voice on radio
during the war years—
with the possible exception
of the Prime Minister. Here
he is with a cup of tea Mrs
Mopp brought him

Worsley saw as Handley's 'feed'), and a mad Russian inventor
called Vladivostooge (Eric Egan). There would be musical
interludes (always a *sine qua non* in old variety shows) played
by Jack Harris and the London Casino Band; there would be a
singer (Pat Taylor); and a couple of regular features—one a
sort of charade, and one a comedy spot in which normal
behaviour would be stood on its head, an applicant for a job
interviewing his would-be employer, and so on.

As to the title—well that, as usual, was a difficulty. After a
great deal of discussion, Kavanagh suggested using a phrase
coined by the *Daily Express* and headlined whenever Hitler
was in the news: IT'S THAT MAN AGAIN, the front page would
declare. And so, the idea having appealed to Eric Maschwitz,
on Wednesday, 12 July 1939, at 8.15 pm precisely, an announcer
was heard to exclaim: 'This is the National Programme.
Ladies and gentlemen—*It's That Man Again.*'

At first, the whole thing seemed a dreadful mistake; no-one

liked the first broadcast, and it was difficult to find anyone who thought much of the second, third and fourth. Then broadcasts from the 1939 Radiolympia interrupted the series, and it seemed doubtful whether the programme would have returned to the air had not Hitler intervened. On Sunday, 3 September, Mr Chamberlain's weary voice announced to listeners that Britain was at war with Germany.

Ever since September 1938 and the Munich crisis, the BBC and its new Director General—F. W. Ogilvie, formerly Vice-Chancellor of Queen's University, Belfast—had realised that war might come, and that if it did, broadcasting would play an enormously important part in it. So preparations had to be made to keep the BBC on the air during the emergency. Among them, were plans for the dispersal of various BBC departments throughout the country. The Variety Department was to be evacuated to Bristol; and it was from Bristol that *It's That Man Again* returned on 19 September. By then, Tommy Handley, doodling on a piece of paper, had shortened the show's title to *ITMA*, and *ITMA* it remained, to become the most popular series of programmes the BBC had yet broadcast.

The success of the programme depended to a very great extent on speed (Handley had always been very quick-tongued), on puns and surrealist use of language, and on the famous *ITMA* door, a brilliantly simple device to introduce comedy characters—a 2ft high property door fitted with a dozen locks and handles, through which they made their exits and their entrances, each actor playing many parts.

It was still to be a while before *ITMA* was to become mandatory listening for almost the entire population of the country. But, already, some of its stars were emerging. One, almost more popular than Handley himself, was a Devonshire man, Jack Train, who played a mysterious German spy whose name was German for 'five'. A telephone would ring, Handley would answer, and out would come the nasal voice, as of someone speaking into a glass tumbler (which indeed was what Train was doing): *'Zis ees Fünf speakink . . .'* It was at the height of the spy craze, when eager eyes scanned the skies nightly for the tell-tale flashing of the white pantaloons of German paratroopers disguised as nuns. Fünf was famous overnight.

Train also played Fusspot, a civil servant who presided over most of the complexities of Handley's Ministry of Aggravation and Mysteries, a brilliant if simple satire on growing red tape in everyday life; and there was also a charlady—Lola Tickle, played by Maurice Denham. Though she 'always did her best for all her gentlemen', she was later to be supplanted by a senior colleague, the totally inimitable Mrs Mopp.

At the end of its first run, though *ITMA* had not overtaken *Bandwagon* in popularity, it was obviously too good to drop. The BBC Variety Department moved on from Bristol to Bangor, and Handley moved with it—to become Mayor of Foaming-at-the-Mouth, surrounded by a new set of characters: Sam, a sort of political secretary, a rather Mafia-type figure, played by Sidney Keith in a voice reminiscent of one of Al Capone's boys: *'Boss, boss, sump'n terrible's happened!'* he would cry, and indeed it always had. Out of doors, on Foaming-at-the-Mouth's seaside strand, Ally Oop, strayed from some Egyptian tourist-trap, sold the dirtiest postcards on the coast; or Handley would be importuned by Horace Percival's diver, announced by a series of bubbles blown by *ITMA's* hard-working effects boy in a cupful of water, and vanishing to the same effect with the words: *'I'm going down now, Sir!'*—perhaps *ITMA's* first universally popular catch-phrase, used by fighter-pilots as they dived on the enemy, by Bevin Boys as they set off for the first time down the mines, or by Londoners as they made for the dubious shelter of the tube stations.

By the beginning of *ITMA's* third series, which started in September 1941, it had become an integral part of the national scene. It will perhaps be impossible for anyone not around at the time to conceive just how popular it was. It sometimes seemed that Hitler could successfully have invaded England on any Thursday evening between 8.30 and 9 pm, and found no opposition: everyone would have been listening to *ITMA*. No radio show since then has had the same impact.

Of course, one or two characters failed to 'catch on'. Few people today, maybe, will have a very clear memory of Comical Chris or Johann Bull, Dr Smack or the Marquis of Mourne. But they were in the minority. Most *ITMA* characters were as well known as the butcher, the baker, or Alvar Lidell: Claude and Cecil (Jack Train and Horace Percival) with *'After you, Claude'*—*'No, after you, Cecil'*; Lefty, a friend of Sam, with 'It's me noives!'; Clarence Wright's commercial traveller, with his cheerful *'Good morning; nice day'*; and of course Mrs Mopp, with her *'Can I do you now, sir?'*—delivered by Dorothy Summers in a plummy, mumsy voice which became one of the show's happiest assets. Poor Miss Summers was dogged by Mrs Mopp for the rest of her life: Arthur Askey remembers seeing her surrounded by autograph-hunters, saying desperately: 'But my name isn't Mrs Mopp. I shan't sign until you say what my real name is.' Alas, nobody knew.

Jack Train introduced Colonel Chinstrap, another of *ITMA's* richest characters, with a voice so thick with alcohol that one fancied one could smell his breath as he greeted the faintest suggestion of a drink with the words, '*I don't mind if I do!*' It was as though the characters were actually vying with each other to provide more and better catch-phrases. Mrs Mopp's '*I've brought this for you, sir!*' or '*TTFN*' was complemented by Ali Oop's '*I go—I come back!*' Mr Wassname (Horace Percival) was so vague he could never finish a sentence; Mark Time answered any query with the words '*I'll have to ask me Dad!*' (though he himself was patently almost a centenarian).

ITMA played right through the war and out at the other end of it. Unquestionably, it faded a little towards the end: the rich early characterisations were replaced by lesser ones—though some of them remain happy memories: Sam Fairfechan, Major Munday and his daughter Naive, Chief Bigga-Banga, and perhaps the most successful later characterisation, Deryck Guyler's Frisby Dyke.

On 5 February 1949, there was a new setting for *ITMA*: Handley was to become the manager of a coffee-stall (providing him with plenty of buns with which to feed Hattie Jacques' endlessly voracious Sophie Tuckshop). But four days later, he died, after a cerebral haemorrhage. I remember the announcement of his death—the leading item in that Sunday's six o' clock news—as keenly as any announcement of war news. The streets of London were lined with people to watch his funeral cortège; ten thousand people were at the crematorium; he was the first comedian for whom there was a national memorial service in St Paul's Cathedral. At the end of a programme broadcast in tribute to him, in a wonderfully imaginative gesture, someone quietly closed the *ITMA* door for the last time.

Several recordings of *ITMA* exist, and very occasionally one is broadcast. They have an enormous nostalgic appeal—but it must, I think, be admitted that they have not worn well. Their topical jokes stale or forgotten, without the culminative effect of being part of a long run, they are simply no longer very funny. Much of the joy with which they were greeted resided in the release of tension they provided for a country tense in muscle and mind with the effort of conducting an apparently almost hopeless struggle. Even if future historians fail to understand the *ITMA* craze, it must certainly be acknowledged that Mr Handley, Sam, Fünf, Colonel Chinstrap, Mrs Mopp and the rest played a not inconsiderable part in keeping up the nation's spirits when they most needed bolstering.

The growing probability of war during 1939 brought various innovations and changes to life in Broadcasting House. One

Joyce Grenfell (*right*)
talking with Lilli Palmer
during rehearsals of *No
Time for Comedy* (1940)—
one of the many programmes
'bringing theatreland to the
troops'

of the earliest was the inauguration, for the purposes of propaganda (though it is doubtful whether the BBC would have admitted that description) of news bulletins broadcast to Europe in French, German and Italian. Other languages were to be added during the course of the war, and the service began which was to become the BBC World Service.

During the Munich crisis there had been a quick flurry of activity at Broadcasting House. Anti-gas doors were fitted, and sandbags hastily piled up in the entrance-hall to ensure the safety of the Archbishop of Canterbury, who came hurriedly trotting in to recite a prayer or two, or to guard from possible blast Major J. F. C. Wickham, explaining in a talk the 'Anti-Aircraft Defence of Britain.'

The new Director General, while as convinced as Reith had been of the godliness and rightness of Britain's posture, was by no means inclined to have the Corporation used as a simple instrument of Government propaganda: he guarded its independence throughout the war, though he co-operated with the Government in general plans for radio—which transmitters would have to be closed down, which amalgamated, which heavily protected against possible air attacks. Wood Norton Hall, near Evesham, was bought for the housing of 600 evacuees from Broadcasting House, and a dog was bought from Battersea Dogs' Home, to parade its grounds at night.

Meanwhile, programmes continued much as usual. The King and Queen came to Broadcasting House in May 1939, to hear Toscanini conduct the BBC Symphony Orchestra. Comedy and dance-music programmes abounded, and Sandy Macpherson, newly appointed, began playing the BBC theatre organ. The only sign of the darkness in the east came during the news bulletins: and, as throughout the war, there was no attempt to minimise the possible dangers or to disguise the gravity of the situation. R. T. Clark, then BBC News Editor, put his philosophy quite simply in a memo which merits a place of honour in the BBC's archives:

> It seems to me that the only way to strengthen the morale of the people whose morale is worth strengthening, is to tell them the truth, and nothing but the truth, even if the truth is horrible.

At one time there had been serious doubt as to whether the BBC could carry on broadcasting in time of war—or, surprisingly, whether it *should*. Within the Corporation itself, however, plans had gone forward to keep the BBC on the air by amalgamating the National and Regional programmes.

At first, news was broadcast every hour on the hour, after the outbreak of war. But this, on the face of it, good idea soon foundered, for a very simple reason—despite Richard Dimbleby doing his best with a mobile recording unit 'somewhere in France', and despite the best offices of unofficial correspondents (there had been no regular BBC foreign news service, and therefore no staff of foreign correspondents) there simply wasn't enough news available for broadcasting.

All types of programmes were to suffer cuts because of the fewer hours of transmission available (123 hours less each week than in peacetime). Talks were cut by 77 per cent, variety by 60 per cent, drama features by 75 per cent. Then, for various reasons, many artistes normally available were suddenly out of reach. The air seemed suddenly to be filled with gramophone records, official announcements (hours of them), and with Sandy Macpherson who, while new recordings and transmissions were prepared in unfamiliar studios in Bristol, Bangor and elsewhere, plodded away at the console of the theatre organ, making twenty-three broadcasts in the first week of the

Eric Linklater (*centre*) was the author of *The Great Ship*, a radio play extolling the courage of British soldiers during the desert war, which was heard three times in one week, in 1943. John Gielgud (*left*) played a leading role, and his brother Val (in many ways the creator of radio drama) produced

war, and twenty-two in the second! Various Government Ministers came to the microphone to give propaganda talks—thirteen by the end of the first week—and what with one thing and another it was not surprising that the BBC's old enemies in the Press began to complain bitterly that this kind of thing was not what a demoralised public needed. There were also complaints in Parliament.

It was not surprising that programming was chaotic during the first weeks of the war, or that gaffes were committed, such as the playing of a melancholy recording of Chopin's *Funeral March* immediately after what was meant to be an inspiring talk by the Archbishop of Canterbury. But within a short time, the heads of the various departments were rethinking their schedules for the months ahead, and planning regular programmes to replace the hotchpotch which was going on at that moment.

As soon as the various producers, actors and musicians connected with the Variety Department heard the radio news announcement that emergency programmes would take over from regular broadcasts, they all—twenty-two of them, with seventeen dogs and a parrot—set out in their various ways for Bristol, where the headmaster's room at Clifton College became the office of the Head of Variety. With all the performers and one orchestra working in a single studio, the Department produced between five and nine programmes a day: an astonishing feat—easy to forgive the fact that the quality was really not very high.

Soon, *Bandwagon* came to the rescue; stars like Gracie Fields appeared in quickly organised special programmes; the dance bands got together again, and in a very short time there were three Bristol studios available to house four bands, including the BBC Variety Orchestra and Billy Ternent's Dance Orchestra. The importance of entertainment was obvious: in what Bernard Shaw described in a letter to *The Times* as 'a masterstroke of unimaginative stupidity', all theatres and cinemas had been closed, and radio was the only cheering medium available to most people. The BBC decided that the evenings should be, more or less entirely, devoted to comedy.

On Monday, *Monday Night at Eight;* on Tuesday (later Thursday), *ITMA*, not yet quite as successful as *Bandwagon*, broadcast on Saturday evening at peak listening time. On Wednesday, the popular *For Amusement Only*, with a variety of artistes, alternated with 'one-off' shows, including a set-piece for Rob Wilton's 'Mr Muddlecombe'. On Thursdays there were popular band shows such as *Henry Hall's Guest Night* and *Songs from the Shows;* Friday was a relatively quiet night, and on Saturday, *Bandwagon* was followed by *Garrison Theatre*,

(*far left*)
Ben Lyon and Bebe Daniels,
with Vic Oliver to complete
the trio, appeared in the only
serious rival to *ITMA—
Hi, Gang!* But Ben and
Bebe were old troupers by
1940: they had not only been
film stars, but had appeared
before the television
cameras, as here, in 1936

A naturalised Englishman,
Vic Oliver, one of the three
stars of *Hi, Gang!*, settled
down after the war to take a
greater and greater interest
in music, conducting his own
concert orchestra and
composing a briefly popular
theme song for it. His career
as a popular comic took
second place to his music
during his last years

devised by Harry S. Pepper and the conductor Charles Shadwell, and compèred by Jack Warner, with Joan Winters as his 'little gel', recitations from blue-pencilled letters from his brother at the Front, and the clatter of his bicycle parked somewhere in the theatre, protected by frequent cries of *'Mind my Bike!'*

Rob Wilton soared to popularity within the first few weeks of the war, simply because he was one of the first comedians really to tackle the crisis head-on as a setting for humour. His attitude to the conflict was simple: he was thoroughly confused by it all, but determined to do his bit—an attitude not so far distant from that of many of his listeners. There must have been some sympathy, too, for his constant attempts to explain to his wife the necessity of his frequent absence from home on duties of national importance:

'The day war broke out', he would explain, he had begun his attempts to help the country out by joining the Home Guard. 'I'm supposed to stop Hitler's armies landing', he told Mrs Wilton. 'What, *you?*' she exclaimed with understandable doubt. 'No, not *me*,' he replied; 'there's Bob Edwards, Charlie Evans, Billy Brightside . . . there's seven or eight of us, we're in a group on guard in a little hut behind the Dog and Pullet . . .'

However *ITMA* fast became *the* comedy show of the war, although others were developing—one of the most popular starring three Americans: Ben Lyon and Bebe Daniels, both well known as film stars, who had lived in Britain since 1936, and Vic Oliver, well known as a comedian (though he had started life as a violinist). He had been born a Viennese Baron, but had given up his title, become a naturalised American, and was now Winston Churchill's son-in-law. The scripts of *Hi, Gang!* were dismal, the jokes elderly and largely pretty unfunny —but the pace was enormous, from Ben Lyon's first *'Hi ,Gang!'* and the audience's reply, right through to his final, *'So long, gang!'* It was the speed that kept the show on its feet.

What kept *The Kentucky Minstrels* on its feet was simple nostalgia and sentiment. The comedy, again, was dismal, but the music struck a note of awe-inspiring sentimentality and religiosity which went down well in the early years of the war. Doris Arnold's sugary choral arrangements of *Abide with Me*, *The Holy City* and *The Lost Chord* seemed completely apposite.

A very different kind of music made Vera Lynn one of the great radio stars of the war. She had made a large number of radio appearances, had been a singer with Ambrose's band, and had made one bestselling record (of *Red Sails in the Sunset*) before the outbreak of war. Then, for the first few months, she appeared on *Ack-Ack, Beer-Beer*—a special series for men

of the Anti-Aircraft and Barrage Balloon units. It was Howard Thomas, a BBC producer, who devised for her a series called *Sincerely Yours*, in which she could be a kind of intermediary between the men in uniform and their families at home.

It was a strikingly simple, strikingly successful idea. The BBC had never before directed messages specifically at individual listeners—except on *Children's Hour*—and it seemed a suspiciously populist thing to do. Basil Nicholls, Controller (Programmes) had rather individual tastes in popular music: he felt that the BBC would be

Ben Lyon and Bebe Daniels rehearse for *Hi Gang!* while Vic Oliver (*foreground, right*) waits his turn. The show survived for a while after the war: this photograph dates from 1949

more in the mood of the moment if we cut out a lot of our dreary jazz sophistications . . . in favour of waltzes, marches and cheerful music of every kind . . . [eliminating] crooning, sentimental numbers, drivelling words, slush, innuendos and so on.

He was not much in favour of Miss Lynn, and indeed his memos, if they had prevailed, would have resulted in the elimination from the air of just what the great majority of listeners wanted most to hear.

Other members of Reith's original upper echelons did not much approve of *Sincerely Yours*, either. It should be said that the country was similarly divided: in the main, readers of the *Daily Telegraph* were on Mr Nicholls' side. The rank-and-file members of the forces were not—and neither were some, at least, of their commanding officers, who believed that the British soldier would fight rather better for home and country after hearing Vera Lynn singing the kind of songs he associated with home, than after a programme of military band music.

Vera Lynn sang directly into the hearts of the forces—particularly those of the men overseas, from whom bad communications kept any news of their families. She would tell them of their newborn children, sing to them of the old familiar things they knew and loved, and with songs like *We'll Meet Again, There'll be Bluebirds Over the White Cliffs of Dover* and *I'll be Seeing You*, she became a vital part of the war effort. (She became completely identified with the songs she sang: I remember vividly a canteen concert during which an adenoidal corporal mounted the stage to announce 'I shall now sing *Yours*, by Vera Lynn.')

She also toured various theatres of war, including Burma, and if MPs talked of 'sentimental, sloppy muck in the Forces programme' (as Vernon Bartlett did), or complained at the 'caterwauling of an inebriated cockatoo' (as Lord Winterton did), few servicemen agreed with them—and neither did the public at home.

There was a certain amount of public wrangling about a good number of BBC radio programmes during the war. Considerable friction resulted, for instance, from the Corporation's attempts to broadcast some of the work of ENSA—the Entertainments National Service Association, which had been set up under the producer Basil Dean to take entertainment to the troops, and to munitions workers. It seems to be true that ENSA was too often the last refuge of tired and worked-out professionals who would have stood little chance of finding employment in peacetime, and Dean did not help matters by insisting that the shows they presented should be at least to some extent 'inspirational' in nature.

The BBC agreed to broadcast *ENSA Half Hour* every week, as well as *Break for Music*, provided by an ENSA troupe moving around the country from factory to factory. But at last Dean's insistence on fanfares, Shakespearean extracts and performances of *Land of Hope and Glory* proved too much for the Corporation. ENSA scripts were rejected as amateurish, and there was a good deal of cattiness between the two organisations.

Regular BBC programmes directed at the factory-worker had considerable success—including *Workers' Playtime*, which began in 1941 as a result of a discussion between the Minister of Labour, Ernest Bevin, and the BBC. A great number of now well known comedians made their first broadcasts in *Workers' Playtime*, which came each week from a different factory canteen 'somewhere in England'. The next most popular light entertainment programme—apart from *ITMA*, *Bandwagon* and *Hi, Gang!*—was probably *Happidrome*, with its regulars, Cecil Frederick, Vincent Robinson and Harry Korris:

> We three, in *Happidrome*,
> Working for the BBC—
> Ramsbottom, and Enoch—and me!

These shows were often produced under great strain: the *Happidrome* team had a journey of about 400 miles to and from Bangor to record a single programme. No-one ever complained, however, and many well-known stars made the long night journey—Cecily Courtneidge and Jack Hulbert, Arthur Askey, Arthur Lucan and Kitty McShane (who for the first time appeared on radio in *Old Mother Riley Takes the Air*).

There were many broadcasts specifically directed at the forces: *Tom, Dick and Harry*, which dealt with the printable adventures of a soldier, sailor and airman off-duty; *Under the Red Duster*, set in the Merchant Navy; *The Blue Peter* and *Ship's Company*. Nostalgia had its moments, not only with Vera Lynn but with Freddie Grisewood in *Your Cup of Tea* (where the clatter of real teacups added verisimilitude), *Home Town* (compèred by the Cockney character actor Ronald Shiner), and many record request programmes like *Over to You* and *Record Time*.

As a result of pressure for more 'informative' programmes, there were one or two more serious projects, including a programme in which no-one had much confidence—*Information Please*, in which a panel of experts would simply answer questions sent in by members of the radio audience. The experts would be carefully selected to provide pithy, entertaining answers, and from a short list of fourteen, three were

chosen—C. E. M. Joad, philosopher and psychologist, Julian Huxley, biologist, and Commander A. B. Campbell, a retired naval officer and anecdotalist; their chairman was Donald McCullough, Public Relations Officer to the Ministry of Agriculture. The programme was to become famous as *The Brains Trust*.

Entitled *Any Questions?*, the programme took the air in January 1941 with a question to which no-one could give a complete answer ('What are the seven wonders of the world?' asked an RAF sergeant). After a few weeks, it became much more a programme of general discussion, and its three main contributors became national celebrities—Dr Joad with his alarmingly literate, beautifully composed spoken essays on this subject or that—sometimes admirably controversial, always stimulating; Huxley with his enormous sense of scientific enquiry and store of knowledge; Campbell with his tall stories (as of his friend who was allergic to marmalade, so that when he ate it, steam rose from the top of his head).

The first series of *The Brains Trust* went on for eighty-four weeks without a break and, after its promotion to a peak time on Sunday afternoons, was regularly heard by 29 per cent of the whole population, receiving between four and five thousand letters a week. It was easily the most popular 'spoken word',

Twenty Questions, chaired by the irascible Gilbert Harding, swiftly became popular, and is still being broadcast. The commentator Richard Dimbleby (*right*) was one of the panellists (later, chairman); so was Anona Winn, who still takes part in the programme

The Brains Trust, which started as a simple programme designed to answer listeners' queries, developed into the most popular informational programmes ever broadcast. Here, in 1941, Quentin Reynolds, Dr C. E. M. Joad and Julian Huxley face, across the table, Commander A. B. Campbell, Donald McCullough, the question-master and E. N. da C. Andrade

programme of the war (excluding the news), and its provocative-ness was part of its charm—the same is true of its rather less literate successor, *Any Questions*, which rather than establishing a small cache of outstanding contributors, calls on a large pool in which the fish are necessarily less impressive.

Apart from the original three members of *The Brains Trust*'s team, others made broadcasting reputations on the programme: Sir Malcolm Sargent, the conductor, was one; Kenneth Clark, Hannen Swaffer, Anna Neagle, Commander R. T. Gould, Barbara Ward and the young Michael Ayrton were others. The programme was criticised, of course—sometimes very ve-hemently, and sometimes from within the BBC. 'The relish with which Joad trots out slick answers to profound questions' was particularly disliked by the Rev J. W. Welch, Director of Religious Broadcasting, for instance (but then, Joad and Huxley were both rationalists). An MP complained of Joad's disgusting language when the latter quoted Confucius: 'What economy is it to go to bed in order to save candlelight if the result be twins?'

But there is no question that the programme was the best combination of entertainment and information yet devised. It remained firmly under the control of the Variety Department until its demise—and it is still remembered with affection and pleasure. Other programmes which hovered between entertainment and information—or straight propaganda—were aimed at listeners on 'the home front': programmes like *Up Housewives And At 'Em*, in which 'Mrs Paper', 'Mrs Metal' and 'Mrs Bone' vied to sponsor the collection of vast quantities of those admirable materials for the war effort ('Script by Harry Pepper, based on the national slogan "Up housewives and at 'em" ', said *Radio Times*). The BBC repertory company of actors and actresses appeared in these little dramas, as well as in plays and features of all kinds, children's programmes and religious services.

Then there was *The Radio Allotment*, broadcast live from the piece of ground industriously dug over by members of the BBC Outside Broadcasts Unit in Park Crescent, near Broadcasting House. Once a week Roy Hay, of the Ministry of Agriculture, spurred listeners on to 'Dig for Victory', with the help of regular broadcasters such as Stewart Macpherson and Raymond Glendenning, the sports commentators. Mr Middleton (he was never known by any other name) became even more famous during the war than he had been before it, with his weekly gardening talks at 2.15 on Sunday afternoons. He was blessed with one of those splendidly calm, ruminative, reassuring radio voices—not unlike the voice of 'the radio doctor', Dr Charles Hill, in the 1950s, whom one remembers giving admirably comforting advice on piles or indigestion—memories which still outweigh his later and more acid moments as Chairman of the BBC.

Other voices dimly echo in the memory: Mrs L. Russell Muirhead on 'Making the Most of Dried Fruit', and Mrs Arthur Webb on 'Making the Most of a Wartime Larder'; Gert and Daisy with awful recipes for nourishing dishes made from reconstituted dried egg. Then of course there were regular ministerial broadcasts—by the Prime Minister, whose talks are part of radio history; by the Minister of Supply, Herbert Morrison (with his two series, *Go to It*, and *Keep at It*), and Lord Beaverbrook urging the workers on to greater and greater aircraft production.

Other areas of broadcasting flourished with what seemed at the time surprising power. The idiocy of the people inside and outside the Corporation who felt that Vera Lynn was a threat to all that was British and Best should not disguise the fact that there was still a very genuine and increasing appetite for classical

Sandy MacPherson supported the broadcasting system almost singlehanded during the first week of the war, when the BBC planners were thrown into disarray. Throughout the war, and until his retirement some years after, he remained extremely popular

music during the war. It is a truism that the arts flourish at times of stress and difficulty and, between 1939 and 1945, regular concerts of classics, and the broadcasting of the Proms, built new audiences. Even the newest works were enthusiastically received—Britten's *Sinfonia de Requiem* and Rubbra's *Fourth Symphony*, for instance; the autograph score of Shostakovitch's *Leningrad Symphony* was brought on microfilm from Moscow, whence it had been flown from the beleaguered city itself. Its reception was enormously enthusiastic.

The first night of the 1940 Proms was interrupted by an air-raid, and nine months later the Queen's Hall was demolished by a bomb. Sir Henry wept among the ruins—and then got on with the business of organising the next series, at the Albert Hall. 'After all,' he said, '*I* am still here'. He continued to conduct through the next three seasons—with the help of some guest conductors; but he was growing old. On the first night of the 1943 season he collapsed, and Sir Adrian Boult and Basil Cameron kept the season going until he was able to return for the last few concerts. The following year, after a masterly account of Beethoven's *Seventh Symphony*, he collapsed again and, a few days later, died. It was the end of the Jubilee

Season, which itself had only been set up with some difficulty: the coming of the V-bomb attacks had led to the suspension of concerts at the Albert Hall, and it had been at Bedford that Wood's last night had taken place.

On 5 June, he had attended a Jubilee Commemoration luncheon, and ended his speech: 'I hope with all my heart that the BBC will carry on my concerts as a permanent annual institution for all time.' So far, that has been done, and there can be no doubt that Sir Henry would approve the present policy of introducing many new works at the Proms—as well as providing complete opera performances and even ballet (though he might not approve the gradual shortening of programmes).

The BBC Forces' Programme, established in 1940, broadcast relatively few of the more serious programmes—indeed, it was condemned by many serious-minded MPs as 'tripe' and 'filth', which was interesting, since by 1942 a far greater number of people in England listened to it than to the Home Service. With the Forces themselves, there was no doubt which service was more popular. When Sandy Macpherson started a Forces Programme request spot in the earliest months of the war, he received 1,500 requests within the first week.

J. B. Priestley—'HE SPEAKS FOR ENGLAND,' said a newspaper headline when Government influence removed him from the microphone for allegedly political broadcasts—delivering one of his famous *Postscripts*, which established him as one of the best broadcasters of his time

Almost as popular, but in a more serious vein, was the novelist
and playwright J .B. Priestley. From June 1940, Priestley made
nineteen broadcasts immediately after the nine o' clock news,
and became, next to Winston Churchill, the most popular
'straight' broadcaster in the country. He precisely caught the
feeling of the public—stout defiance, a wry humour and a touch
of sentiment. His scripts were written with great professionalism
—simple but forthright, sometimes elegaic. One of the best
known celebrated the 'little ships' which had set out from Eng·
land to rescue the defeated BEF from the beaches of Dunkirk :

> Yes, those Brighton Belles and Brighton Queens left that
> innocent, foolish world of theirs to sail into the inferno, to
> defy bombs, shells, magnetic mines, torpedoes, machine-gun
> fire, to rescue our soldiers. Some of them—alas—will never
> return . . .

One of the seaside steamers which was sunk was the *Gracie
Fields*, which used to ply between the Isle of Wight and the
mainland.

> But now—look!—this little steamer, like all her brave and
> battered sisters, is immortal. She'll go sailing proudly
> down the years in the epic of Dunkirk. And our great·
> grandchildren, when they learn how we began this war by
> snatching glory out of defeat, and then swept on to victory
> may also learn how the little holiday steamers made an
> excursion to hell and came back glorious.

Such stuff, of course, was quite irresistible : Mr Priestley
was not an oustanding popular novelist for nothing. But his
broadcasts were less than rapturously received in some quarters.
He was a declared Socialist, and hints of his political stance
were seen in some of his statements. Some members of the
Coalition Government—Mr Churchill, it is rumoured, among
them—became extremely hostile, and, in October 1940,
Priestley was taken off the air. None of his successors, who
included Robert Donat and Leslie Howard, the actors, and
A. P. Herbert the writer and MP—who to his discredit made a
political attack on Priestley—had the same success.

In January 1941, Priestley reappeared at the microphone
for another series of *Postscript*. A deputation of Conservative
MPs immediately protested, and the Prime Minister himself
complained that Priestley's first broadcast seemed to indicate
that the author's war aims were not those of the Government
(Priestley had taken the line of argument that Britain should be

'aggressively democratic'; Mr Churchill obviously thought that rather dangerous—never in his own successful broadcasts to British listeners had he actually detailed his own war aims). Once more, Priestley was virtually banned from the air, and though his voice became familiar to American listeners, he never again broadcast during the war exclusively to the British.

During the London blitz, broadcasters found themselves under the same pressures as anyone else whose business took them every day into the centre of the city. Portland Place was right at the centre of things; even if it was not a specific target for German bombs (which it may well have been), it was well battered. The staff had formed a well drilled Home Guard Section right at the beginning of the war. The main news studio was moved to the sub-basement, and heavily protected; the Defence Room was guarded by armed men, and a notice posted announcing that anyone failing to show a proper pass would be shot on sight.

Bomb damage was considerable. St George's Hall, with the BBC theatre organ, was destroyed on 25 September 1940 (fortunately during one of the rare occasions when Sandy Macpherson was not present). On 15 October, there was a direct hit on Broadcasting House itself, with seven people killed. As the bomb crashed through the top three floors of the building, Bruce Belfrage was reading the news. There was a quiet thud, a whisper, and then the bulletin continued. Not far away, a bomb demolished the building next to a studio from which a variety show was being broadcast. Claude Dampier fumbled a cue, repeated it more steadily, and the show went on.

The landmine which exploded in Portland Place on 8 December caused considerable damage too: fires burned in Broadcasting House for seven hours, and many members of the staff remained on duty for several days without a break, sleeping in wrecked offices or in nearby Egton House until order was restored. Outside the main doors an armoured car waited every evening ready to drive announcers to studios in Maida Vale if broadcasting became impossible from the usual studios. Tickets were issued for beds in the Concert Hall, where a curtain of blankets insecurely divided men from women. But broadcasting was never interrupted.

At the same time, radio set before the country—and before the world—the sufferings of Londoners, Plymouthians, the people of Coventry under blitz. *London After Dark* and *London Carries On* were broadcast during air raids, with, in the background, the sound of the guns trying to fight off the bombers. *The People of Coventry* was broadcast soon after the centre of that city was decimated. *Spitfires Over Britain* and *Balloon Barrage* told the story of the battle of Britain, and *Bombers Over Berlin* of retaliation on the German capital. In what was considered a typically English manner, there was some concern that there should be no note of pride or gloating in the voices of commentators describing the shooting-down of enemy 'planes, or the dropping of bombs on enemy cities.

Though the BBC, probably rightly, had no great confidence in the power of propaganda, several overtly patriotic broadcasts were transmitted; but the estimated sizes of audiences for various programmes tell their own tale—almost eleven million people (according to the *Yearbook* for 1940) heard *Bandwagon* and *Garrison Theatre* on Saturday nights; seven million listened to *War Commentary*—a military broadcast by Major General Sir Ernest Swinton—and six million to *American Commentary*. Five million regularly tuned to a programme officially sponsored by the Ministry of Food, telling people 'what to eat and how to cook it'; two and a half million listened to the Wednesday symphony concert, and a million and a quarter, as a matter of course, to evening prayers, broadcast on three evenings a week.

On the doleful Christmas Day of 1940, at the darkest point of the war, the BBC mounted a programme no doubt calculated to appeal to world sentiment: it was called *Children Calling Home*, and during it youngsters evacuated to Canada and the USA sent messages to their parents. *Children under Fire*, which preceded it, told of the adventures of the less fortunate ones who had been forced to remain in Britain (though in the end, who knows, they may have been the more fortunate).

Then came *Christmas Cabaret*, which (as Asa Briggs points out in his massive *History of Broadcasting in the United Kingdom*) provided a microcosm of the whole year: Arthur Askey and 'Stinker' Murdoch, Elsie and Doris Waters and Jack Warner (incidentally, their brother) provided the fun, Geraldo played dance music, John McCormack, the popular tenor, sang, Adrian Boult conducted some Mozart, and Ernest Bevin appealed for wireless for the blind.

By now, new names had been added to the roll-call of famous radio personalities: the names of hitherto anonymous BBC announcers. It was John Snagge who organised the change: he decided that for various reasons—not excluding the fact that the Germans, invading Poland, had had great success with fake news bulletins read by actors imitating Polish news readers— names should now be put to voices. So one day in 1940, listeners heard the words: 'Here is the news, and this is Alvar Lidell reading it.'

Lidell was deputy to Stuart Hibberd, the chief announcer

(who had joined the old Company on its second birthday). His parents were Swedish, and he had joined the BBC in 1932 after various other jobs. An amateur lieder-singer and keen darts-player, he spoke several languages fluently. Frederick Grise-wood (who, always announced as 'Freddie', was to chair *Any Questions* for over twenty years until his retirement at the age of seventy-nine) became a BBC announcer in 1929, had originally been a singer, and was a goodish comedian—he created a rustic Cotswold character called Old Bill, who broadcast occasionally.

Then there was the Devonshire Frank Phillips, another professional singer who had appeared at Bach Choir and Royal Choral Society concerts before becoming an announcer in 1935. Lionel Gamlin had been President of the Cambridge Union, and was probably better known as the compère of *In Town Tonight* and *Puzzle Corner* than as a newsreader. Wilfred Pickles, a Northerner, somewhat irritated the Establishment by reading the news in his native accent; after the war, his *Have a Go* was to be a great success. Roy Rich was a latecomer to announcing after a career as production manager with Moss Empires. He later became a TV executive.

The announcers seem, in retrospect, to have had a dull and dispiriting war, bringing news of fresh disasters sharp at nine o'clock every evening. No wonder that one of them, coming to the microphone with a news script containing details of the battle of Alamein, was heard to announce: 'Here is the news—and some cracking good news it is, too!'

BBC news broadcasts were avidly heard in Europe as well as in Great Britain. Broadcasts to France were particularly important. *Ici la France* was regularly broadcast from 1940 onwards, with Jean Masson commenting on current affairs. After Pétain's capitulation, General de Gaulle made the first of several broadcasts from London to the French people, and some magnificent French broadcasters appealed to the spirit of France throughout the remainder of the war. Churchill also spoke to France on several occasions: '*C'est moi*, Churchill, *qui vous parle.*' he began in the execrable French which was all the more appealing to his listeners. Perhaps many among the crowds who greeted him in Paris not long after the liberation remembered those broadcasts, as a great roar of laughter and applause followed the opening words of his speech on a balcony overlooking the Place de la Concorde: '*Prenez garde—je parle Français!*'

As the war went on, radio was increasingly used, not only as a first-rate medium of propaganda (which included quite simply the accurate reporting of war news, either concealed or

During the war, BBC equipment was developed so that outside broadcasts could take listeners into the front line at home and in Europe. Here, the microphone records an interview with a Bofors gunner in a coastal ack-ack battery 'somewhere in England'

distorted by German radio), but as a means of conveying secret messages to underground workers in the occupied countries. There were also highly successful broadcasts to Germany itself.

War reporting during the days of the battle of Britain was fairly limited; but as soon as British forces went overseas, the BBC began to send its commentators out to the various war fronts, and they did very remarkable work under some difficult and dangerous conditions. As early as 1941, Bruce Anderson reported from South Africa on the battle of Mahda Pass, Richard Dimbleby from Keren and from Addis Ababa as Haile Selassie returned as King—the first leader of a state to be returned to his position after being temporarily removed by the Axis.

New names were heard: Chester Wilmot, of the Australian Broadcasting Service, broadcast from the Western Desert, as did Edward Ward (until his capture by the Italians). They often worked under difficulties not all of which stemmed from the war: the BBC's administrators at home, as Dimbleby knew all too well, were extremely good at making life as difficult as possible for correspondents working in conditions of which they knew nothing.

One sound seemed above all others to dominate the air during the war: a sound which still makes it difficult to listen, thirty years later, to the opening of Beethoven's *Fifth Symphony* without memories quite alien to that work.

During a broadcast to occupied Europe on 14 January 1940, a Belgian broadcaster, Victor de Laveleye, suggested that the

letter V was one which might happily be used as a symbol of coming victory—it stood not only for the English word, but for the French *victoire* and the Flemish *vrijheid*. Within a few days, news was leaking through from the Continent that not only in Belgium but in France and Holland, the letter V was appearing chalked over Nazi posters, or painted on walls. In March, the BBC received a letter which said that in Marseilles so many Vs had appeared that there was 'not a single space on any wall, without one'. In April, Radio Paris announced that anyone caught painting a V anywhere would be prosecuted and landlords were warned that they would be responsible for any Vs painted on their property.

Any slogan which got so quickly under the skin of the Nazis was obviously worth encouragement and, despite the risk of provoking reprisals, the BBC and the British Government decided to promote it. When 'Colonel Britton' (Douglas Ritchie, a BBC assistant news editor) began broadcasting to Europe in June, the morse sign for V (. . .—) was used to introduce him (it had been specially recorded by the timpanist Jimmy Blades). The first theme of the Beethoven *Fifth Symphony*, which fortuitously uses the same *motif*, followed the morse signal. That drum-beat became, from late June, the identification signal used by all broadcasters to the Continent. Teachers were encouraged to teach their children to clap it; people were encouraged to tap it out over the telephone; prisoners in Nazi prisons tapped it on the waterpipes which connected their cells. . . .

In England Vs appeared everywhere—mostly unofficially, but sometimes erected by authority, as in Leicester, where a V was placed on the clocktower of the town hall. Churchill gave the V-sign with two fingers on every possible occasion—to the delight of the troops, to whom it meant something quite different (the old man, cannily, was fully aware of the popular obscene significance of the gesture!). If there is some reason to believe that the V-sign campaign was self-defeating in occupied Europe, it should certainly not be forgotten that at its height, in 1941, it added greatly to the somewhat manic gaiety with which Britain was putting her shoulder to the wheel.

By the time D-Day arrived, both technicians and broadcasters had attained a degree of professionalism which was to enable the closing year or so of the war to be more fully reported than any other event in human history until that time.

There was very careful planning, in top secrecy, of the BBC's schedule for D-Day. A special lightweight recorder (it weighed 40lb!) had been devised by BBC engineers, and plans were

Radio went into battle for the first time soon after D-Day (though other battles, in the Western Desert and in Italy had been less comprehensively covered)

made for getting the records (there were as yet no tapes) and written reports back to Broadcasting House as quickly as possible.

Two days after the relief of Rome came the news of the allied invasion of Europe. At 9.30 am, John Snagge read to the people of Europe a text issued by General Eisenhower, in which he asked resistance leaders to carry out the instructions which they had previously been given. The King of Norway and the exiled Prime Ministers of the Netherlands and Belgium broadcast in their own language.

Gradually, news reports began to filter through from the Normandy beaches: the one o'clock news included an eye-witness account, from an aircraft, of the invasion, and after the nine o'clock news came a new programme—*War Report*—which in the next few months was to be followed anxiously by up to fifteen million listeners. For the first time it included informal reports from the very centre of the fighting—including an extraordinary recording in which an RAF officer apologised for breaking off his description of events: 'I don't think it's much good trying to do these flash running commentaries when you're doing a dive-bombing attack.'

War Report was the first really modern news magazine programme; in its own time, it was the most ambitious news programme yet broadcast. Perforce, its editors and compilers used ingenuity, speed and nerve combined with accuracy and immediacy, and the result blazed a trail which led reporters on through the crises of the smaller wars to come, until the art of war reporting has become as fully professional as modern warfare itself.

The new standards of speed and accuracy in reporting had their critics. Field Marshal Montgomery protested that the BBC was putting his men in danger by revealing the state of battle to the enemy, and General Bradley also believed that over-accurate reporting had cost the lives of American soldiers. The British Press returned to its pre-war sport of criticising the Corporation, violently jealous of the number of BBC correspondents in Europe, and of their superior organisation.

But now the war was over. The BBC's correspondents, who had provided such a marvellous service to listeners at risk of their own lives, came home: Chester Wilmot, Godfrey Talbot, Stanley Maxted and Frank Gillard were some of them. In some ways, 1939–45 had been radio's greatest years, just as the decade to come was to signal the beginning of the end of radio's triumph and the rise of television. As the battle for Europe ended, the battle for the survival of radio as a creative medium was beginning.

Murdoch and Horne disregarding pressing problems at the Air Force Station at *Much-Binding-in-the-Marsh* to pay attention to the News. 'These sets take a very long time to warm up', Murdoch would say, as Horne pipped and whistled and tootled in the background . . .

V Normal Service will be Resumed

During the war, the BBC had learned a great deal about two areas of broadcasting—news and comedy. Strangely enough, the fact that enormous listening-figures had built up for the nine o' clock news each evening did not prompt the Corporation to take advantage of this to make news the centre of their radio operations. That was to come much later, when radio was driven to the point of desperation by the popularity of television. Even so, improved techniques of news-gathering and presentation made the News much more lively and immediate.

'News features' became more common, for instance. In peacetime, there was not quite the motive for listening which had given programmes like the 1943 *Victory in Africa* (about the battles in Tunisia) audiences of several million. But the News itself continued to command the attention of a large number of people—not perhaps the 50 per cent or so of the entire population which had listened in wartime, but still a large proportion. The difficulties of the late 1940s were considerable enough to give many people the impression that the war—or *a* war, at least—was still being fought; as indeed it was.

It was probably this fact that brought so many listeners to the radio comedy programmes which followed *ITMA, Hi, Gang!* and the other wartime shows. Some comedy programmes trundled straight on into peacetime: *Merry-go-Round* and *Much-Binding-in-the-Marsh* were two of them. The first, starring Eric Barker, had started life as a navy show, the latter, with Richard Murdoch (of *Bandwagon*) and a newcomer, Kenneth Horne, had originally been a comedy show aimed especially at the RAF.

Merry-go-Round was originally the generic title of a series of three shows which alternated, week in, week out—the third was a show which Charlie Chester hosted for the army (and he too was to have his own popular peacetime show a little later). *Much-Binding* was certainly the most popular, and in some respects the best of the three, depending on the happy combination of Murdoch and Horne.

The original idea had set up the Laughter Command of the RAF, and a ramshackle air station called Much-Binding-in-the-Marsh, where the inmates gave battle to all the frustrations of inconvenience and red tape that war had laid upon them. In peacetime, *Much-Binding* simply turned itself over to non-combatant operations. The two stars were their own script-writers. Both were Cambridge men—Murdoch with all the experience of *Bandwagon* and a career in showbusiness, and Horne, a minister's son, basically a businessman (they had been, in fact, in the RAF together, and as Wing Commander Horne and Squadron Leader Murdoch had spent a great deal of the war writing comedy scripts; and who shall say that was not a work of national importance?).

Sam Costa, formerly a singer and later a good disc-jockey, had also been drafted into the RAF, and eventually found himself working as batman at *Much-Binding*, with his muffled enquiry *'Was there something?'*. He also played Prudence Gush, the radio critic, when Much-Binding became a weekly newspaper, *The Weekly Bind*, with Dora Bryan as Gladys Plumb, its fashion editor.

Much-Binding was said to be King George VI's favourite

Richard Murdoch and Kenneth Horne presided over several more or less loony establishments during the war. Here, at the microphone, are (*left to right*) Diana Morrison, Kenneth Horne, Richard Murdoch, Sam Costa and Maurice Denham (in *Over to You*, 1952)

show, after the death of Tommy Handley put an end to *ITMA*. Eric Barker's *Merry-go-Round* catered for a rather more intellectual taste; he relied on brilliance, satire and wit rather than on simple situation comedy. Barker had started life in his father's business, and had written several short stories and three novels before 'going on the stage' where, at the Windmill Theatre, he met his wife, the dancer, Pearl Hackney.

Barker had been in the navy during the war, and started the nautical section of *Merry-go-Round*. His wartime radio naval base, HMS *Waterlogged*, became in peacetime *Waterlogged Spa*, and in the last year of *ITMA's* life (when that show was fading a little) it actually gained larger listening figures on one occasion. Barker was another writer/performer, and *Waterlogged Spa* was full of good characters, though they never managed to be quite as memorable as the *ITMA* crowd. There was the First Lord of the Admiralty, for instance, an ex-dustman who owed to the newly elected Socialist Government his appointment to high office. (Later he was to become Baron Waterlogged.) His daughter Phoebe (pronounced Feeb) was one of those odd radio characters who became very well known, though never actually heard.

Jon Pertwee, who appeared regularly with Barker and Pearl Hackney, made a national hero of his little Devonshire postman —once a burglar at Plymouth barracks—with an equivocal attitude to letters ('*What does it matter what you do as long as you tear 'em up?*'). Then there was Humphrey Lestocq as Flying-Officer Kyte, the archetypal ex-RAF officer with handle-bar moustache and a fake university accent of proportions only believable to those who had heard some of the originals. Barker himself, driven to distraction, maintained great calm, only occasionally when on the edge of panic breaking out with his own catch-phrase, '*Steady, Barker!*'

The third of the *Merry-go-Round* shows was *Stand Easy*, the army show, originally written by Sergeant Chester of the Royal Irish Fusiliers. Chester was an experienced comic (he had made his first stage appearance at the age of seven at the Winter Garden, Eastbourne). Before the war, he had been 'on the halls' as a sort of pale shadow of that great comedian Max Miller (whose own material was mostly too blue for him ever to make much of an impact on radio, to the eternal sorrow of those who considered him without question the funniest man of his generation).

'Cheerful Charlie' Chester made *Stand Easy* a music-hall show, with the help of Arthur Haynes (later a great television comedian), Len Marten, song-writer Ken Morris and singer Fred Ferrari, whose ear-splitting tenor fulfilled amply the

Jon Pertwee, one of the stalwarts of *Merry-go-Round*, appeared in various unfamiliar guises, not the least obscure being that of thirteenth trombonist in the Waterlogged Spa Symphony Orchestra (1947)

criteria of listeners who regarded the tenor voice as an instrument the excellence of which could be judged in direct proportion to its volume.

These were the three top comedy shows of 1945–48, though there were others which, like them, survived for a while from war into peace. They varied from the good (*Up the Pole*, with Jimmy Jewell and Ben Warris; or *Happidrome*) to the frankly awful (*Factory Canteen* and *Works Wonders*) in which the 'entertainment' was provided by the workers themselves. But there were others to come: and the greatest of these was originated by two men who, according to Peter Black in his *The Biggest Aspidistra in the World*, first met in a cinema in Regent Street.

The film was a drama set in period France. The hero was drinking in a café, drowning his sorrow because his girl had left him.

'Do not worry,' said a friend; 'she will come back.'

'No', replied the hero; 'women are different than men.'

'Ah', said the older man, 'Monsieur is a philosopher!'

(*far left*) Charlie Chester's *Stand Easy* rivalled other comedy shows in the ratings during the late '40s. *Left to right*, Roman St. Clair, Arthur Haynes (later a great TV comedian), Ken Morris, Len Marten and (*almost out of the picture*) Chester himself

(*below*) Charles Maxwell, the producer, holds the microphone in a heavily posed publicity photograph of the *Take It From Here* team. The programme, written by the new team of Denis Norden and Frank Muir (*front row*), became the natural successor to *ITMA* as radio's leading comedy show, with, as its stars, Jimmy Edwards, June Whitfield, Alma Cogan and Dick Bentley

Only two people in the audience laughed. They were Frank Muir and Denis Norden.

Ted Kavanagh, the writer of *ITMA*, used them on a number of different shows, one of which was an entertainment called *Take It From Here*, first broadcast on 23 March 1948, and not doing at all well. It was an unambitious sort of programme— sketches, songs, band numbers—and the performers (certainly they could not be called stars) were Jimmy Edwards, Dick Bentley and Joy Nichols.

Bentley was the most experienced: he had come to England from Australia before the war, and had made his first broadcasts then. During the war he toured with Australian Army concert parties, and when he came back to England in 1947 met Edwards and Joy Nichols during a guest appearance on *Navy Mixture*—another wartime show, on which the latter was then working. Jimmy Edwards was an ex-chorister of St John's College, Cambridge; he had been a Flight Lieutenant in the RAF during the war, earning the DFC and being shot down over Holland. He went into show business after the war because there seemed nothing better to do: like Eric Barker, he underwent a period of battle training at the Windmill, where comedians had to fight to keep the attention of rows of men who were only there because it was the one theatre in London where they could see completely nude girls (albeit they were not allowed to move).

The third member of the triumvirate, Joy Nichols, was another Australian, once a child prodigy in Australian radio (a fate quite as bad as serving for a year at the Windmill), and now hoping to make a living in London. The prospect was dim until the advent of Muir and Norden: but then *Take it from Here* took off, and became the most popular radio programme of its time, and a classic, if that term can be applied to any radio programme.

As in so many cases, it was coincidence that set the show off on its wave of popularity. When Tommy Handley died, the BBC was faced with the prospect of filling not one but three half-hour spots (the show had two repeats each week). One of them, on Saturday lunch-time, was given to *Take it from Here*— and, fortunately, the particular edition which filled the first of those spots was a good one. Within a year, the show had won the *Daily Mail's* national radio award as the best show of 1949.

From the moment Muir and Norden got their hands on it, *Take it from Here* began to change the route of radio comedy. It no longer, for instance, relied simply on a 'stand-up' routine or a situation. It began, certainly, with a piece of chat between the three stars—an ordinary gag routine, if you like. But then

it went on to a satirical sketch on some topical news item, and ended with a burlesque of a film in which the writers would indulge their taste for excruciating puns (a taste subsequently turned to good account in *My Word*), but at the same time reduce the film formula for romance, period drama, or social drama to the *n*th degree of absurdity.

Dick Bentley, June Whitfield, Jimmy Edwards and Alma Cogan, the stars of *Take It From Here*

This was all very well and good, as growing listening figures proved; but it was the invention of the Glums, in the early 1950s, which made *Take it from Here* immortal. Mr Glum, a loudmouthed boor (Jimmy Edwards) presided over a household consisting of his ever-absent wife (nothing but a distant voice, very obviously that of Edwards himself in non-visual drag), his son Ron, who was not even one degree removed from utter idiocy, and was played with sublime incoherence by Dick Bentley, and Ron's fiancée Eth (June Whitfield, a magnificent radio comédienne) whose famous catch-phrase was a plaintive *Oh Ron!* Each week, poor Eth was foiled in her attempts to rise to a richer and happier life (as promised by the small ads in the *News of the World*) by the utter opacity of Ron, and the

121

One Minute Please (1952) was the predecessor of *Just a Minute*. A women's team (Margot Holden, Violetta and Martina Mayne) opposed a men's team (Frank Muir, Philip Harben and Gerard Hoffnung—the cartoonist and originator of the humorous musical festivals). Roy Plomley (obscured by the microphone) was the chairman

cupidity of his father. Time after time, just as she seemed to have coaxed Ron into some more or less gallant display of wooden affection, Mr Glum would burst in with his '*Ullo, Ullo, Ullo . . .?*' as though seduction was imminent—when it was all too plain that Ron only recognised one end of poor Eth from the other because one end had feet on it.

The Glums became national figures beside which prominent politicians, churchmen and showbiz celebrities were but pale shadows. Occasional repeats of episodes from their saga only prove their superiority to anything else going on in the comedy line during their time.

Not that other comedy shows were not extremely popular in their own way. Nedlo, the Gypsy Violinist, for instance, started his own show on 4 April 1949, and made a very considerable success of it. *Ray's a Laugh* did not actually include Nedlo's name among the credits, nor indeed that of Charlie Olden (his real name). Nedlo/Olden was, by 1949, calling himself Ted Ray—and that was how he billed himself for his new radio series.

His earliest ambition, he has said, was to be either the Prince of Wales or a cowboy; despite his father's years in showbusiness as a character comedian, Ted started work for a cattlefood manufacturer—work from which he soon escaped to

122

become a member of the Ainsdale Football Club team. Then, for a while, he was a ship's steward, then a violinist in a dance band (his violin-playing has been compared favourably with that of Jack Benny).

Finally, the variety stage claimed him and, as Hugh Neek (he seems to have had a rare talent for awful names), he sang parodies of popular songs of the day, working mostly in cinemas. In the 1930s—by which time he had settled on his final, 'real' stage name of Ted Ray—he had his first taste of real success, and by 1932 was playing the London Palladium as a stand-up comic. In 1939 he first broadcast in *Music Hall*, actually managing to make the same audience laugh twice at the same jokes (the first recording having proved unusable because of a technical hitch).

It was in 1939 that the BBC had the idea of setting up a Crazy Gang of the air (a sort of counterpart to the stage *Crazy Gang* in which Flanagan and Allen, Nervo and Knox and the rest had been so successful). War broke out after the first broadcast. During the war, Ray made several broadcasts, and was more than ready in terms of experience and radio technique, when his main chance came with *Ray's a Laugh*.

He had decided years before to break away from the red-nosed comic tradition, and had made his success as an ordinary

Ted Ray, an extremely experienced broadcaster, was in style very close to Tommy Handley; and when Handley's death ended *ITMA*'s long run, *Ray's a Laugh* (with Kitty Bluett as Ray's 'wife') took over

Laidman Browne, a 'straight' radio actor who played many roles in radio drama, was Ted Ray's boss, Mr Trumble, in *Ray's a Laugh*, on the BBC Light Programme

man in an ordinary lounge suit, whose jokes had a real basis in everyday life. Naturally, his radio show was in the main a domestic comedy (his wife was played by yet another Australian, Kitty Bluett). Ted Yule, and later Kenneth Connor, played his brother-in-law, and the rest of the cast was, or were, Peter Sellers, then only twenty-three and billing himself as 'an impressionist'. Music was supplied, with frenetic enthusiasm, by Bob and Alf Pearson, and by John Hanson, later the star of so many musical-comedy revivals.

Another early member of the cast was Patricia Hayes (a straight actress whose work since *Ray's a Laugh* has included playing Tony Hancock's landlady, Mrs Cravat, and giving an award-winning performance in the brilliant television feature *Edna, the Inebriate Woman*.) She appeared as a strange lady called Crystal Jellybottom (*'Stop it, you saucebox!'* she would cry in a crazy soprano). Charles Leno and Graham Stark, both later to do fine work in radio, were also present.

The show was not any kind of real departure from the traditional, even in its catch-phrases (but then, even *Take it from Here* had its catch-phrases). There was Ivy's (Ted Ray) devotion to Dr Hardcastle, for instance: *'He's loovely, Mrs*

Hardcastle, he's loovely!' And it was she to whom another character would remark, weakly, *'It was agony, Ivy!'* Then there was the adenoidal *'If you haven't been to Manchester, you haven't lived . . .'* *Ray's a Laugh* ran from 1949 until January 1961—a long run; and *Ted Ray* still shows his extraordinary skill at ad-libbing (together with Jimmy Edwards, Arthur Askey and Cyril Fletcher) in *Does the Team Think.*

On the face of it, the one radio show of 1950 least likely to succeed was one which was broadcast for the first time on 6 June, and starred—a ventriloquist! A ripple of incredulity ran around the offices of the BBC when the idea was first mooted, though in America the ventriloquist's dummy, Charlie McCarthy, had had a successful radio show for twenty years, and the Corporation had no inhibitions about copying American ideas. It just seemed very much against the odds that an act which depended to such a degree upon an audience watching a dummy's lips move when a ventriloquist's did not, should succeed on radio. Well, sceptics were soon to be proved wrong.

Peter Brough was a ventriloquist's son. Like Arthur Askey, he made his early reputation and living playing 'the masonics', and though he had an audition for radio as early as 1938, it

On 14 November 1947, BBC radio celebrated its 25th birthday, and some of the men and women who had been involved from the days of 2 LO took part in a celebration broadcast: *(left to right seated)*, Harold Nicolson, Wynford Vaughan Thomas, Mabel Constanduros, Stuart Hibberd, John Snagge and Ted Kavanagh; *(standing)* Mona Dinwiddie (a programme engineer), Francis Worsley (producer), Harry Morris (programme engineer) and Michael Barsley (producer)

Educating Archie starred a ventriloquist's dummy—Archie Andrews—but was one of the most popular comedy shows of the '50s. Here, Peter Madden, Hattie Jacques (a stalwart of radio comedy) and Robert Moreton, the first of Archie's tutors, stand at one microphone, with Peter Brough, and the dummy Archie, at the other

seemed fairly obvious that there was no future in his act in a non-visual medium. Fortunately, he did not *need* success to the extent that other performers did: at the age of 23 he was already running his own successful textile business. During the war, in the RASC, he gravitated to the world of forces' entertainment, and after he had been invalided out, gave some time to improving his act. It was at that stage that he came up with the idea of a new dummy: a schoolboy with an atrociously grating treble voice, which was matched by a perky face with prominent eyebrows and the slickedback hair of the period. Ted Kavanagh only had to set eyes on it, to know how to introduce it to its creator: 'The name,' he said, 'is Archie Andrews.'

Brough and Archie were booked for a single *Music Hall* appearance. It was a great success, not only with the studio audience but on the air. There was still a twelve-month interval, however, before a second radio booking—in *Navy Mixture*. That was also a success, and this time, the producer, Charles Maxwell, decided to take a gamble and book Brough and Archie for a regular spot in the show—to be called *Archie Takes the Helm*. Ted Kavanagh wrote the script with Sid Colin, who had written *Hi, Gang!*

126

That was during the later stages of the war: after *Navy Mixture* ended, there were regular radio appearances, but Brough—with one eye on Charlie McCarthy's success—had set his ambition rather higher, and, with Sid Colin, worried the BBC to give him his own show. A trial pilot was made, with Bonar Colleano (well known on radio and also in films) and Jon Pertwee. It was a flop. Brough was disconsolate, but in 1948 returned to the charge with an idea for a show starring himself and the brilliant impressionist Peter Cavanagh ('The voice of them all'). That was a mild success, and a little later the producer, Roy Speer, arranged another pilot based on a new idea of Brough's—for a show in which the main theme was to be Archie's education.

That was really rather impressive, the programme planners thought; and though they only scheduled *Educating Archie* for a six-week try-out, with the option of a further six weeks, they did pay Brough the compliment of scheduling the new show for the spot formerly filled by the phenomenally successful *Take it from Here*. The fact that Sid Colin, as writer, was now joined by Eric Sykes, was nothing but a gain, and by the end of the initial twelve-week run, *Educating Archie* was holding a regular audience of twelve million people. Brough and Archie were offered marvellous contracts by major theatre impressarios, and Radio Luxembourg promised them £1,200 per programme if they would come over to the opposition. The BBC countered with a three-year contract, which Brough accepted, and the show ran on for thirty weeks without a break, with Robert Moreton as Archie's tutor, Max Bygraves as an odd-job man, and Hattie Jacques in various supporting roles. A young girl soprano, only thirteen, was the resident singer. Her name was Julie Andrews.

Educating Archie is another case of the radio show which took over the country in a way no radio show is likely to do ever again. Kiddies licked Archie Andrews lollipops and washed themselves with Archie Andrews soap; there were Archie Andrews comics and annuals, and the dummy's face appeared everywhere (for charity as well as for enviable fees).

After its first break, the show returned with a new tutor: a comedian who had been popular with listeners to *Variety Bandbox*—one Tony Hancock. Then Max Bygraves (who had had the show's best catch-phrases, '*That's a good idea—son!*' and '*I've arrived, and to prove it I'm here*') left, and Alfred Marks took over. When he left, Gilbert Harding briefly took his place. Beryl Reid and Harry Secombe appeared in the third series (when the show once more won the *Daily Mail's* award). During musical interludes, Ronald Chesney played on his harmonica.

Meanwhile, other stars were emerging. Radio was a voracious medium—there was so much time to fill. Frankie Howerd was by now helping to fill it, though it was not until the 1960s that he was to be recognised as a comedian of real and individual genius. Al Read had less original technique, but great talent for satire in his brilliant improvisations on everyday life. Read had been a professional travelling salesman, and his observation was as sharp as a razor-blade, and as dangerous. His impersonations of policemen or elderly ladies of less than prepossessing humour, were magnificent (as was his small boy at the theatre, fixing his evil eye on an insect perched on the bald head of the man in the seat in front. 'You want to go to heaven, little fly?'—SWOT!—'You've gone!') His catch-phrase 'Right, monkey!'—whatever that may have meant—became as popular as any of the *ITMA* phrases.

Then there was *In All Directions*, with Peter Ustinov and Peter Jones—perhaps the most sophisticated radio comedy show of its period; and Eric Barker continued his good work in *Just Fancy*, with a wonderful comic set-piece for two elderly gentlemen (himself and Deryck Guyler).

What a wonderfully rich period of radio comedy listeners enjoyed between the end of the war and the late 1950s! And

The birth of *The Goon Show:* youthful-looking Peter Sellers, Harry Secombe and Spike Milligan with the bearded Michael Bentine in one of the earliest programmes of the long-running series (1951)

there were to come, now, as natural successors to *Take it from Here*, two of the most successful radio comedy series ever broadcast: one of them starring one of Archie Andrews' tutors, Tony Hancock, the other with four men listeners had barely heard of—though two of them had vestigial radio experience, Peter Sellers in *Ray's a Laugh* and Harry Secombe in *Educating Archie*. The third man was Spike Milligan, the fourth Michael Bentine, an old Etonian, and the show was *Crazy People*, later to become *The Goon Show*.

The three men who became famous as the Goons (Michael Bentine appeared only in the first few shows) were in fact widely disparate characters, though with the same extraordinary sense of humour, and with an enthusiasm for comedy which was to carry them on through the long series. Together, they made an unbeatable team.

Harry Secombe, a Welshman with a piercing tenor voice which he developed, without professional training, into an instrument which he can now use to considerable effect in 'straight' songs, was yet another graduate of the Windmill. He had made several radio appearances during and after the war, and in 1950 was sharing a small London flat with Spike Milligan.

Harry Secombe (*centre*), with Max Geldray (the harmonica player who took part in most of the *Goon Shows*) and Spike Milligan; an anonymous actor (*left*) looks somewhat bemused, as well he might

Milligan was born in India (he made a splendid contribution to a notable feature series in 1975, *Plain Tales from the Raj*). During the war, in his early twenties, he played the trumpet in various forces' ensembles, and also for the first time discovered a real talent for making people laugh. One day, in North Africa, Lance Bombadier Secombe was sitting with his detachment at the bottom of an escarpment on top of which gunners were digging in. One of the guns was prematurely fired and, recoiling, bounded down the slope within feet of Secombe's tent. Shortly afterwards a face appeared round the tent-flap. 'Anybody seen a gun?' it plaintively enquired. So met Secombe and Milligan—later to share the same ward in a convalescent hospital. In peacetime, Milligan became a member of the Bill Hall trio, with comedy taking second place to trumpet-playing, and with a talent for script-writing gradually showing itself in material he wrote, with Jimmy Grafton, for the comedian, Derek Roy, in whose show *Hip-Hip-Hoo-Roy* he also appeared.

Peter Sellers was the only Goon with real theatre experience. He had gone into showbusiness at the age of eighteen, and during the war appeared (mainly as a drummer) with ENSA and later with Ralph Reader's *RAF Gang Show*. After the war came a spell at—yes, the Windmill Theatre. By now, Sellers' talent as an 'impressionist' was quite clear, and he proved it by telephoning a BBC producer in the persons of both Richard Murdoch *and* Kenneth Horne, to recommend himself. The producer was sufficiently impressed to give him an audition, and he made his first broadcast in July 1948.

It was Jimmy Grafton who brought the Goons together and, after a couple of pilot shows which met with no great enthusiasm, the BBC was sold the idea of a zany comedy series which, though first billed as *Crazy People*, soon became (as a result of internal pressure), *The Goon Show*. It was, and remains, an extremely odd title—the word 'goons' first appeared in Popeye cartoons long before the war, was American gangsterese for 'tough guy', and was finally used by RAF prisoners-of-war when speaking of their captors. It has never been clear why Sellers, Milligan, Secombe and Bentine were so fond of it.

The early *Goon Shows* were infinitely more conventional than the later ones. There were the usual sketches, with musical interludes (from the Ray Ellington Quartet and the harmonica-player Max Geldray, who lasted for almost the entire series). The subjects were everyday: satire on politics, the Festival of Britain (this was 1951), even the BBC itself. But already the germ of *Goon Shows* to come was busy; Milligan, for instance, was experimenting with involved sound effects.

The pattern was very much that of other radio shows: the

first broadcast, on 28 May 1951, was followed by a contract for six more, then for a further six, then five more. But, contrary to folk-memory, *The Goon Show* was not an immediate roaring success. Only a million and a half listeners had been collected by the end of the first series, and they did not seem to be extraordinarily enthusiastic. But the audience was to mount steadily. The second series—of twenty-five programmes—saw it rise to three million; and by now regular listeners were making friends with some of the Goons' classic characters— the divinely simple idiot Eccles, Colonel Bloodnok, Minnie Bannister and her infinitely aged lover Henry Crun.

Gradually, the format of the show changed too—instead of a series of sketches, there were single-subject shows (the first was *Crun Up the Amazon*); and in the third series, which started in November 1952, a new producer, Peter Eton, took them further along the line, and the familiar Goonish titles made their first appearance: *Fred of the Islands*, *The Mystery of the Cow on the Hill*, *Where Do Socks Come From*, and *The de Goonlies*.

Eton, by all accounts, played a very considerable part in the growing success of the Goons. He had been a features and drama producer, and apart from instilling a certain amount of discipline into the anarchic conditions in the studio, he was also able to contribute to the presentation of the show—so that, as Roger Wilmut has pointed out in his *The Goon Show Companion*, it actually sounded as though it was a slice of some kind of weird life, rather than a recording made in a BBC studio.

With the fourth series (which ran for thirty episodes, from 2 October 1953) there was another step forward: recordings were for the first time made on tape, which enabled the Goons to *ad lib* as much as they liked, secure in the knowledge that anything too outrageous could be cut from the programme before it was broadcast. Pre-recording of most radio programmes has removed most of the tension from sound broadcasting— in many cases a great loss; but in the case of the Goons, the gain was considerable, for some of their eccentric, surrealist flights of humour took wing to such effect that they heightened the style of the whole series.

By now, too, *The Goon Show* had settled down as a series of episodic, picaresque adventures of hero Neddie Seagoon, whose companions Bluebottle, William 'Mate', and Hercules Grytpype-Thynne were to make an unbeatable team. Bluebottle (Peter Sellers) was to become as indispensible a character as Spike Milligan's Eccles, to be greeted with a round of applause at their first lines in each script.

It was in 1954 that the popularity of *The Goon Show* began to reach epidemic proportions, and part of this at least was due

In a St David's Day issue of *The Goon Show*, the Goons (Milligan, Sellers, Secombe) strike a leek

to a one-off programme written by Milligan (who by now was writing the scripts for the programmes in collaboration with Eric Sykes). This was *The Starlings*—an account of an effort to rid Trafalgar Square of a plague of those birds. The programme was recorded as though it was a feature, with no audience; but from the start it was clear that the whole thing was taking place in Goonland. The firing of rice puddings from catapults was only one of several schemes which were tried, and failed, before Jim 'Tigernuts' Bluebottle conceived the splendid notion of artificial explodable bird-lime, which did the trick.

The programme was a classic; and as with other great radio occasions, drew considerable attention from the upper echelons of BBC bureaucracy (the Corporation always maintains on its staff a certain number of people who can be relied upon to keep an echo-image of Victorian Auntie alive). Not only had an imitation of Richard Dimbleby been used during the show (commentating on the spectacle in Trafalgar Square through a Great Gold Microphone of State), but Peter Sellers' Duchess of Boil de Spudswell sounded uncannily like Her Majesty the Queen. It is said that John Snagge led the inter-departmental *Goon Show* protection unit which saved the trio from having

their contracts cancelled—though the threat can have been no surprise to them; attacks had been made on the series from within the Corporation, from its inception. The Goons managed to stay just the right side of what the BBC regarded as permissible bad taste, though a ban was imposed on Peter Sellers' spectacularly good imitations of Winston Churchill.

By now almost every *Goon Show* was a classic of its kind (and although, again, one must hesitate to use that term, there are certain programmes which no other will fit). From *Dishonoured, or the Fall of Neddie Seagoon*, through *The Raid of the International Christmas Pudding* (1956), *The Histories of Pliny the Elder* (1957) and *The Spon Plague* (1958) to *I was Monty's Treble* and *The Childe Harolde Reward* (1959), each programme had its memorable situation and lines. The programme broadcast on 23 February 1959 was meant to be the last: but the uproar from listeners was too much for both the Corporation and the Goons (there were demonstrations, petitions, banners . . .) and another series of six programmes was produced. But *The Last Smoking Seagoon*, broadcast on 28 January 1960, *was* last of the series, though there have been various runs of repeated recordings of the best of the

The visual gags used by the Goons in the broadcasting studio (here Secombe, Bentine, Sellers and Milligan inspect the ceiling through wine glasses) frequently convulsed the studio audience, but left the radio listeners wondering whether they had missed a verbal felicity. With the speed at which those kept coming, they probably had

programmes, and in 1972, as part of the Corporation's Jubilee (or, as Spike Milligan contended, the anniversary of Lord Hill's legs—'They've been together now for fifty years') *The Last Goon Show of All* was recorded in front of a royal and distinguished audience.

The Goon Show was from the start the thinking man's radio comedy: it relied on that kind of humour which from Edward Lear and Lewis Carroll onward depended on a capacity to recognise the absurd as an integral part of life, and then to drive that recognition to the point of hysteria. Henry and Minnie, in their flat at the top of the Albert Hall, were not simply as 'real' as Arthur Askey and 'Stinker' Murdoch in their flat at the top of Broadcasting House; they were so absurd as to be, in a sense, more believable. Min and Henry have been seen and heard too often on the tops of Number 88 buses to be wholly fictional.

The marvellous sound-effects—still more ambitious than anything any other radio show has tried—were certainly an ingredient to catch the listeners' attention; so were the idiot Goonisms—'*Ying-tong-iddle-i-po*' (which became the chorus line of the popular song *I'm walking Backwards for Christmas [across the Irish sea]*), '*needle-nardle-noo*' and '*yuckabakaka*'.

But the stars were, of course, Milligan, Secombe and Sellers —Milligan not only for the scripts, but for Minnie, Moriarty (the villain of the series) and the beloved Eccles; Secombe for Neddie Seagoon (in a sense the weakest of the trio, but often apparently the most beloved of the audience—perhaps because he lacked the manic nervous tension sometimes very apparent in the other two), and Sellers for an amazing number of characters, including Gryptpype-Thynne, Bloodnok and Mr Crun.

Not that one thought of these characters as 'played by' the Goons: they were themselves—they had a life of their own— and no wonder that, in the scripts, their lines were prefaced not by MILLIGAN (Minnie), but simply by MINNIE, a lady in her own right. Even the characters who appeared only occasionally had a three- (some would say four-) dimensional existence, bolstered by absolutely unforgettable names: Councillor Major J. D. Windermere Ropesock, QC, has a kind of immortality conferred by his name alone. And as for the major characters: well, they rank with—who?—Robin Hood?— Lawrence of Arabia?—Mr Gladstone?

Major Bloodnok was one of the first to catch on with listeners, no doubt because he appeared in the earliest programmes. Based on an Indian Army major Sellers had encountered during the war, Bloodnok was distinguished by towering incompetence, endless cupidity, and a digestion evidently ruined by long service in the East (*'No more curried eggs for me!'* he would cry, after one of Milligan's most imaginative 'noises off'). He had a small group of accomplices—Major Throat, for instance, of the strangulated vocal chords, Abdul and Singhiz Things; but his main attachment was to Neddie Seagoon, who had once, it seems, been his batman.

A large scoutmaster with a high treble voice had been the inspiration for Bluebottle, Sellers' major and most beloved creation. Introduced at first by recorded applause suddenly terminated before his opening lines, Bluebottle soon no longer needed the record nor found it easy to stop the applause. The epitome of all schoolboy heroes, Bluebottle, alas, had his career terminated (*'You have deaded me!'*) in almost every show, which is not altogether surprising, for he was apt to dash rashly into the most dangerous situations armed only with his cardboard cut-out catapult. Seagoon took the most outrageous advantage of him, subjecting him to shock, shell, dynamite and high water.

Bluebottle became a bosom friend and companion of the equally attractive Eccles, Milligan's splendid dumb ox of a man, created long before *The Goon Show* was thought of. Roger Wilmut has compared him to Walt Disney's Goofy, and the comparison is extremely apt. The friendship between Bluebottle and Eccles is one which reached heights of idiocy rarely paralleled in English drama. Here is just one exchange between them:

BLUEBOTTLE: What time is it, Eccles?

ECCLES: Um, just a minute. I got it written down here on a piece of paper. A nice man wrote the time down for me this morning.

BLUEBOTTLE: Eug! Then why do you carry it around with you, Eccles?

ECCLES: Well, um, if anybody asks me the time, I can show it to them.

BLUEBOTTLE: Wait a minute Eccles, my good man . . .

ECCLES: What is it, fellow?

BLUEBOTTLE: It's written on this piece of paper—what is eight o' clock, is writted.

ECCLES: I know that, my good fellow—that's right, when I asked the fellow to write it down, it was eight o' clock.

BLUEBOTTLE: Well, then, supposing when somebody asks you the time it *isn't* eight o'clock?

ECCLES: Well, then, I don't show it to them.

BLUEBOTTLE: I wish I could afford a piece of paper with the

	time written on. Here, Eccles—let me hold that piece of paper to my ear, would you? . . . Here, this piece of paper ain't going!
ECCLES:	What? I've been sold a forgery!
BLUEBOTTLE:	No wonder it's stopped at eight o' clock. You should get one of them things my grandad's got. His firm gave it to him when he retired. It's one of them things what it is that wakes you up at eight o' clock, boils the kettle, and pours a cup of tea.
ECCLES:	Oh, yeah—what's it called?
BLUEBOTTLE:	My grandma.
ECCLES:	Ah. Here—wait a minute—how does *she* know when it's eight o' clock?
BLUEBOTTLE:	She's got it written down on a piece of paper.

My own favourite characters apart from the immortals just mentioned (and those most people spent most time imitating—for a great many people in Great Britain, including HRH the Prince of Wales, spent some time conversing in Goonese) were Henry Albert Sebastopol Queen Victoria Crun, and his—well, one must not offend Mr Crun's susceptibilities, but perhaps paramour is the only word—his paramour, Miss Minnie Bannister, saxophonist and ex-follower of the Indian Army. Various halfhearted attempts were made to convince listeners that Miss Bannister and Mr Crun were man and wife; but they were unconvincing. Their aged, creaking voices, punctuated by long pauses during which strange sounds like mice in old wainscoting issued from their throats, punctuated many later *Goon Shows*.

Grytpype-Thynne and Moriarty became dual villains, though the former started life as a suave playboy type. Moriarty was nothing but a villain, given to such Milliganesque exclamations as '*Sapristi Bombetts!*'. His apotheosis as the Dreaded Batter-Pudding Hurler places *The Murders in the Rue Morgue* in the children's bedtime-story division as to horror.

Neddie Seagoon, the 'hero' of the series, was played by Secombe in an enthusiastically melodramatic style, and was ever-optimistic, however insane the plot into which he was drawn. He entered into plans to insure the English Channel against fire, or to export snow to the Sudan, with equal enthusiasm. But he remained human, in a way which other characters in the show failed to copy (even the announcers, first Andrew Timothy and then Wallace Greenslade, became dehumanised in a most un-BBC-announcer way). In a sense, Secombe held the shows together rather as Kenneth Horne, a little island of sanity in a weird world, stood at the centre of *Round the Horne*, later.

Almost a decade after the last of the series, *The Goon Show*s live, the characters as memorable as ever. When the proceedings of the House of Commons were first broadcast in 1975, the *Daily Mirror* accurately suggested that it sounded like nothing so much as an OB of some strange meeting in Mr Crun's drawing-room, with the reservation that the Goons would have been funnier.

It was on 2 November 1954 (three years after the first broadcast of *Crazy People*) that *H·H·Hancock's Halfhour* had its first broadcast. Hancock was then thirty years old. He had had his first job at Hector Powe's, the tailor, in Birmingham. It lasted for two hours and thirty-five minutes. Later, he became a civil servant, and also made his first stage appearances, another imitator of the great Max Miller, earning ten shillings a time. Drafted into the army during the war, he had some experience with ENSA and in Ralph Reader's *Gang Shows*; after the war, he made his way inevitably to the Windmill, and there did a one-man impression of a seaside concert party.

He auditioned for the BBC, and broadcast in some *Workers'*

The most comprehensively funny radio, and later television, comedian of his time, the incomparable Tony Hancock (here at the microphone with Kenneth Williams, Bill Kerr and Sidney James, who with Hattie Jacques made an unbeatable team)

Playtime programmes, and then in *Variety Bandbox*. He was, by all accounts, pretty dreadful. But in 1951, he appeared in a show called *Happy Go Lucky*, starring Derek Roy; and his material was written by two young scriptwriters who had met some months earlier in a TB sanatorium on the Isle of Wight. That mysterious alchemy which had drawn the Goons together worked with Alan Simpson and Ray Galton. They became so necessary to Hancock that when, years later, he turned away from them, he found his genius deserting him, and slid rapidly down-hill to a tragic death.

But, in 1951, the magic began to work—though not at first with Galton and Simpson. Hancock was cast as Archie Andrews' tutor in *Educating Archie*, and scored a great success (his catchphrase, '*Flippin' Kids!*' seems embarrasingly weak now, but caught on immediately with listeners). As a result of his success, he played in revue in the West End with Vera Lynn and Jimmy Edwards, and appeared in the Royal Variety Command Performance with Gracie Fields and Gigli!

Then, Dennis Main Wilson, who was producing a series called *Forces All Star Bill*, decided he wanted a resident comic, and invited Hancock to play; the show was renamed *Hancock's Halfhour*.

With Hancock were three men who were to become his familiars for the whole series; Sid James, the most splendid foil, Bill Kerr, and Kenneth Williams. Later, Hattie Jacques joined them. The series started slowly, but then gained momentum, and by 1955 Anthony Aloysius St John Hancock of 23 Railway Cuttings, East Cheam, was firmly established in the affections of millions of listeners.

Hancock, Galton and Simpson were responsible, from the start, for the format of the programme. It was not to be a programme of comedy sketches and gags, but a situation comedy more like a half-hour play than anything else. It was without musical interludes or other interruptions, and centred on Hancock as a recognisable character with his own behaviour-patterns and foibles. Sid James was assured where Hancock was insecure, forthright where Hancock vacillated. James had never appeared on radio before, and according to Galton and Simpson was terrified at the prospect, literally shaking with nerves at recording sessions, and wearing an old trilby well pulled down over his eyes to hide his face from the audience.

Main Wilson had seen Kenneth Williams playing the Dauphin in a revival of *St Joan*, and Bill Kerr had worked with Galton and Simpson before. Hattie Jacques, who had worked with Tommy Handley in the last series of *ITMA*, was to become housekeeper, friend and butt of the team.

Inasmuch as he had an occupation at all, the Hancock character was a failed actor (he went off on one occasion, I seem to remember, to repertory in the North Country to give his Hamlet—which was naturally to be played in the manner of the late Robert Newton as Long John Silver, parrot and all). His pretentions, snobberies and prejudices were dragged to the surface and eagerly explored, and their expression was so outrageously funny that one laughed at them, and, in laughing, perhaps forgave them in him and in others. As Hancock put it in a *Face to Face* interview on television:

The character I play isn't a character I put on and off like a coat. It's a part of me and a part of everybody I see. . . . You take the weaknesses of your own character and of other people's characters, and you exploit them. You show yourself up, and you show them up.

Well, Hancock had his weaknesses. His tremendous *tours de force* in radio (think of the *Sunday Afternoon* episode, punctuated by such adventurously long pauses that one thought the cast had gone home) were taken on into television; but then his daemon drove him too far. He had, he felt, gone as far as he could go along one particular road. He must go on and on, outward and upward into new fields of comedy. He dropped Bill Kerr, then Sid James and the rest of the team. Then he decided to part from Galton and Simpson. After that, everything he did failed. He made two abominably bad series for ITV, and two indifferent films. He began drinking heavily (he had always been a heavy drinker), and was unable to cope with the frustration which dogged him—his character had become so well defined that audiences would not allow him to succeed at anything else. In Sydney, Australia, on 25 June 1968, he died of an overdose of sleeping pills. He was only forty-four.

Hancock and the Goons were fighting a brilliant rearguard action for radio against the mounting and inevitably successful opposition of television, and both managed to build and maintain a very large audience. The last radio comedy show to do this was *Round the Horne*, the successor to *Beyond Our Ken*, which had started in the late 1950s. Both programmes revolved around the sane, everyday character of Kenneth Horne, a man too upright, amiable and likable to be a part of anything in the least disreputable. Or at least that was the first impression. But as one listened, it became perfectly clear that Barry Took and Marty Feldman, the writers, had placed him at the centre of a whirlpool of outrageous suggestiveness never before

Patric Dickinson, whose poetry programmes on the BBC Home Service were sensitively compiled and well produced, here goes over a script with the young Welsh poet Dylan Thomas (later to write the radio classic *Under Milk Wood*)

(*Right*)
Mervyn Johns, one of the many Welsh actors who made the original recording of Dylan Thomas's *Under Milk Wood*. He played Willy Nilly Postman, and is seen with the producer and only begetter of the piece, Douglas Cleverdon (1963)

tolerated at Broadcasting House. (Years later, Barry Took was able to ask Sir Hugh Greene, then Director General, why on earth *Round the Horne* had been allowed to continue. 'Well,' said Greene, 'to tell you the truth, I rather like a good dirty joke.')

Dirty, or merely grubby, off-colour or glaring scarlet, the jokes were undoubtedly good; and so were the characters. Took and Feldman, who created them, were really television writers (in those days, when people still moved from television to radio, rather than the other way round). They had created *Bootsie and Snudge*, an extremely entertaining ITV series for Alfie Bass and Bill Fraser. Then they wrote the short *Beyond Our Ken* series, and eventually *Round the Horne*, which continued for seventy shows, until Kenneth Horne's sudden death.

Splendid though the scripts were, once more it was the alchemy of good casting which made them a success. Kenneth Williams, by now well known from *Hancock's Halfhour*, moved over to join Hugh Paddick, Bill Pertwee and Betty Marsden as regulars. Williams' many and eccentric voices came in useful for several characters: he played, for instance, Rambling Sid Rumpo, the itinerant folk-singer—whose songs, allegedly collected from the hedgerows and byeways of Old

England, were full of heavily accented allusions to strange physical attributes such as goolies and groats, futtocks and moulies, while the choruses were sufficiently equivocal as to be capable of almost any interpretation:

> Rollock me fusset
> And grindle me nodes,

he would sing, to the delight of his audience, whose feeling was that somewhere beneath the surface there lurked wells of indecency whose depths could only be guessed at; and maybe they were right.

Williams also played Chou en Ginsberg (MA, failed), a fiendish Japanese, and J. Peasemould Gruntfuttock, a crazed old gentleman whose prediliction for Festival of Light attitudes was doomed to be disregarded by the rest of the cast. But perhaps his happiest creation was Sandy, who with his bosom companion Julian, played by Hugh Paddick, explored new regions of 'camp'. Jule and Sand were named after those two admirable musical comedy composers Julian Slade and Sandy Wilson (whose own opinion on the characters has never, as far as I know, been canvassed).

Originally, they were two elderly actors down on their luck and driven to cleaning house for anyone who cared to pay; but later they became two gay middle-aged men-about-town, whose adventures never ceased to amaze 'Mr 'Orne'. One week, they might be running a male boutique ('Here's a nice paisley army-style battle-dress jacket. . . . We call it Aldershot Camp'); next week, a firm of caterers ('Just give us a free hand and we'll give you a do your guests will never forget.')

Then there were Dame Celia Molestrangler and Binkie Huckaback, a couple of elderly romantic actors who seemed always to be appearing in old-fashioned romantic drama, and whose dialogue was nothing unless one could hear their voices—as rich as fruity port. Betty Marsden and Hugh Paddick played them as to the manner born.

Though there have been other attempts at comedy on BBC radio—notably perhaps *Hello, Cheeky!* and *I'm Sorry, I'll Read That Again*—the era of great radio comedy ended with *Round the Horne* (Kenneth Williams' attempts to find a new format for his own enviably forceful radio personality have so far been comparative failures). The really giant audiences have deserted to television, taking with them the great comedy scriptwriters. Though the stars are still prepared to play for radio (a couple or even three radio programmes can be recorded on one day, as opposed to the long sessions for recording one

TV programme; so the economics are reasonable), writers can no longer spend time writing for radio when an equivalent amount of time writing a TV script brings much greater rewards. Now, most radio comedy comes from TV scripts loosely and often carelessly adapted—though, exceptionally, the transition sometimes works well, as with the popular *Dad's Army;* and one must except, too, *The Men from the Ministry*, written by Edward Taylor and John Graham for those two stalwarts Deryck Guyler and Richard Murdoch.

It is a pity, as radio can still be a marvellous medium for comedy, and when one talks to comedy scriptwriters they show keen interest in the medium and its possibilities. But they have their income-tax to pay. Sadly, it's a question of money.

VI One, Two, Three, Four...

On 29 July 1945, the BBC officially returned to peacetime working. The Forces' Programme became, inevitably, the Light Programme; the Home Service was joined once more by the various regional programmes; and Sir William Haley, the Director General, promised that sooner rather than later there would be a Third Programme, which would be devoted to more mind-stretching fare. The Home Service, broadly speaking, came to reflect the everyday preoccupations of the ordinary listener. The Light Programme provided 'entertainment' in a remarkably broad sense, and the Third broadcast programmes of minority appeal. The earliest months of the Third produced some spectacular and, then, even 'dangerous' productions such as Sartre's 'blasphemous' *Huis Clos;* and there was a *Twelfth Night* for instance, with Jimmy Edwards as Sir Toby and Beryl Reid as Maria. The Third also began its patronage of a new generation of young dramatists—Harold Pinter, N. F. Simpson, Samuel Beckett, Alun Owen.

Sir George Barnes, the first controller of the Third, was a man of great vision and tenacity of mind. He was responsible for planning its first great landmark—eighty-three broadcasts on *The Ideas and Beliefs of the Victorians*. His successor, Harman Grisewood, kept up the high standard in music as well as drama—both *Don Pasquale* and *Man and Superman* were given in uncut versions. In those early days, there were eleven Ibsen plays, and Bertrand Russell and Dr Coplestone discussed, unscripted, the existence of God.

Alas, in time, this great concept in broadcasting was to be watered down until what had been the splendid Third died on 3 April 1970. Many listeners and many broadcasters still mourn it.

144

Radio Four, meanwhile—or the Home Service, as it was then
—had built up a splendid audience for drama, with the help
of a great generation of radio actors, including Gladys Young,
Laidman Browne, Carleton Hobbs, Marjorie Westbury,
Norman Shelley and others. This radio repertory company
drew audiences of over ten million for performances in *Saturday
Night Theatre*.

Under Laurence Gilliam, Features continued the work it had
been doing during the war, and rose to new heights. Small
masterpieces of radio such as Henry Reed's and Donald Swann's
Hilda Tablet saga led towards radio's perhaps most famous
single drama production, Dylan Thomas' *Under Milk Wood*.
At the time of his death in 1953, Thomas had for various
reasons (only some of them literary) become probably the best
known poet writing in English. He had made his first broadcast
in 1937, and although his radio work was mainly for the Welsh
Region of the BBC, his reputation as a broadcaster grew steadily,
and (apart from his apocalyptic readings of his own and other
people's poetry—programmes which he and Edith Sitwell
presented between them were among the most remarkable
poetry programmes of their period) such talks as *Quite Early
One Morning*, *A Child's Christmas in Wales* and *A Visit to
America* were truly memorable. Gilliam's Features Department
was, intellectually at any rate, the glory of the post-war BBC, and
its achievements have still to be equalled. Between 1949
and 1955, all the radio programmes submitted by the BBC for
the Italia radio prizes were from Features, and between 1947
and 1955 every single Italia prize for drama was won by that
department.

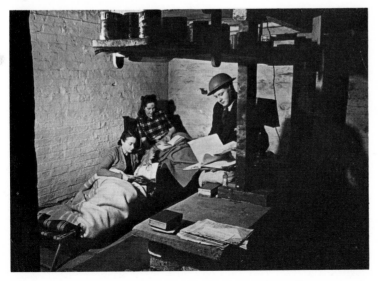

Like other organisations
remaining in central London,
the BBC had its
underground shelters during
the war. In one of them, in
1941, Mary Allen, Marianne
Helweg and Laurence
Gilliam (the brilliant
producer of memorable
radio features) read through
a script

After the war, a spate of serials brought tough guys and detectives to the microphone: here, Leslie Perrins, Duncan McIntyre, Marjorie Westbury and Kim Peacock rehearse an episode of *Paul Temple and the Curzon Case*

Regular BBC productions were holding much larger audiences spellbound. There were, for instance, the popular soap operas—*The Robinson Family*, *Mrs Dale's Diary*, *The Archers* (started as a farming instruction programme) and *Dick Barton, Special Agent*.

Dick Barton, in one's memory at all events, took over the country much as *ITMA* had done. It was also the first really effective serial (only *The Robinson Family* pre-dated it). The idea of a daily drama thriller was proposed by Norman Collins,

146

Head of the Light Programme, on New Year's Day, 1946. After considerable argument about style, production and casting, *The Devil's Gallop* introduced Episode One at 6.45 on 7 October that year—and Noel Johnson's voice was first heard as he led his intrepid colleagues 'Snowy' White and Jean Hunter into peril ('Jock' Anderson was to appear a little later).

Apart from the comedy shows discussed in the last chapter, the Light Programme had other successes, making stars of two performers whose popularity was almost unprecedented:

Dick Barton—Special Agent became a folk-hero to a whole generation of schoolboys (and an amusement to most of their parents) in the late '40s. Noel Johnson (*left*) played Barton, with Alex McCrindle and John Mann as his stalwart henchmen, Jock and Snowy

at least, this was so in the case of Wilfred Pickles, the star of *Have a Go*. Perhaps Vera Lynn, during the war, had had the kind of success which came now to another singer—Donald Peers, a Welshman, who had left Ammanford when he was still a boy. Wilfred Pickles was a star of a different kind, yet with the manifest attributes of friendliness and warmth which helped to lift Peers in his career. Pickles, born in Halifax, began to broadcast in the 1930s as an actor for Northern Region, and during the war he was brought to London as a national newsreader. The Minister of Information had felt that the 'voice of the people' should be heard from Broadcasting House, and Pickles had never had what might be called a 'BBC voice'! It was just after the war that it was suggested that he might like to compère a radio quiz game—an unscripted programme

Donald ('By a Babbling Brook') Peers, radio's 'Cavalier of Song'

which would involve the man-in-the-street. *Have a Go* was the title he himself suggested.

Unscripted programmes—almost unknown before the war—were now more and more commonplace; so were radio games such as *What's My Line, The Name's the Same* and *Twenty Questions* which is still running, no doubt by popular request. Such programmes—like the many discussion programmes and 'chat' shows—have, of course, the advantage of being reasonably cheap; panellists receive their fee, so does the chairman; but there are no expensive musicians to pay, no supporting cast. And at their best—in, say, *My Word* or *My Music*—they can be, given the right 'mix' of panellists, extremely entertaining.

Gradually the News Division of the Corporation grew more and more powerful, eroded more and more air-time, until in

In the late '40s and through the '50s, Wilfred Pickles took *Have a Go* to church halls throughout the length and breadth of the land, 'bringing the people to the people.' It was all good, homely fun, as this picture shows

Jack de Manio, introducing the early morning show *Today*, became a familiar radio character. His later series, *Jack de Manio Precisely*, recalled by its title his unfailing capacity for misreading the studio clocks

the 1970s *Today* (a lightweight news magazine programme) accounts for two hours' broadcasting every weekday morning, *The World at One* for half-an-hour at lunchtime, and *PM* an hour every evening from 5 to 6 pm. The result is, of course, a great deal of repetition of news stories, a frenzied stealing of stories from newspapers, and a sprawling rather than tightly efficient news service—there simply isn't enough news to go round, and the welcome provision of background to the news is too often sacrificed to trivia or sensation.

News makes its own stars. *Today* was for years introduced by Jack de Manio, a sometime announcer with personal idiosyncracies, but who stamped his own personality on radio with an unmistakable effect. The most notable event of his early career was a boob of unprecedented proportions, when, at the time of the Independence of Nigeria, he introduced 'a talk by Sir John MacPherson on "The Land of the Nigger".' Since he left the programme, Robert Robinson, one of the most intelligent broadcasters working in the medium, and Brian Redhead (who also chairs *A Word in Edgeways*, the best discussion programme on radio) have also made successes in his chair.

The other life-size star of news and current affairs programmes was the ex-Fleet Street editor William Hardcastle,

who was employed by radio to introduce *The World at One* and *PM*. His personal style could be extremely irritating, but he was unquestionably a 'character', at a time when radio was growing increasingly short of them.

If the revolution in the presentation of news is one of the most effective areas of post-war broadcasting, and the introduction of the Music Programme—an extention of the Third Programme to daytime broadcasting exclusively for classical music—was another, in a sense the rise of pop music and the eventual birth of Radio One was, quantitively, the greatest revolution of all.

By the 1960s, the BBC's attitude to pop music was giving rise to extreme irritation among those listeners whose life revolved around it. Perhaps it simply did not occur to anyone interested in pop that they were likely to get much satisfaction by tuning to the BBC at all. So it occurred to a young Irishman Ronan O'Rahilly, that it might be a very good idea to set up his own radio station, from which pop could be broadcast without restriction. This meant, of course, that the radio station had better not be in any position to be restricted; and that in turn suggested that the only place from which it could operate was international waters. The pop pirate stations were about to be born.

Radio Caroline anchored 5 miles off Harwich on Good

One of the few real stars of radio news was ex-Fleet Street editor William Hardcastle, whose fine nose for news and breathless way of conveying it made *The World at One* and *PM* compulsive listening

Friday, 1964, and at 9 pm that night began broadcasting test signals. On Easter Sunday, Simon Dee introduced 'your all-day music station', broadcasting pop music between 6 am and 6 pm every day of the week. Radio Caroline was joined two months later by Radio Atlanta, and soon the combined stations were claiming an audience of seven million (technically all law-breakers, for it was against the law to listen to unlicensed radio transmissions).

The situation became farcical and eventually extremely nasty when gang-warfare broke out between the pirates: there was minor and major espionage, suspicion of blackmail and murder. Big money was by now involved.

But whatever machinations were going on, in smoke-filled rooms, the pirates were heard. Listeners liked the music, the new, free style of broadcasting; and the pirates felt fairly secure. But they overplayed their hand: foolishly, they did not take the precaution of ensuring that their broadcasts did not interfere with, for instance, radio distress signals—let alone the wavelengths allotted to radio astronomy. There was a powerful outcry against the inaction of the Government. The full story of the internecine warfare between the stations, the battle between them and the Government, the political, managerial and financial plots and counter-plots, cannot be told here, fascinating though it is. The point, as far as radio is concerned, is that by the time the Marine Broadcasting (Offences) Bill became law in 1967, a very large audience indeed had had its taste for pop fed and cultivated to an extent the BBC had never envisaged. Their radio future seemed dim: they may even (as Lord Sorendon had alleged in the House of Lords) have felt 'desolation in their hearts'.

But the BBC was to come to the rescue. On 3 March 1968, Radio Caroline South ceased broadcasting when she was boarded by real Dutch pirates, who ripped the electrical equipment out as a disc-jockey was speaking. Six months earlier, on 30 September 1967 (by which time most of the pirates had been silenced), the BBC introduced Radio One.

In July of that year, Frank Gillard, the Director of Radio ('Sound Broadcasting' as a term had now been dropped) announced that the radio channels Home, Light and Third would in future be known as Radio Four (the old Home Service), Three (the old Third), and Two (the Light Programme as far as its musical content was concerned), and that a new channel, Radio One, would broadcast a service of pop music. The advent of Radio One marked a radical change, and it was signalled when the Corporation announced the names of the disc-jockeys placed under contract.

Most of them were out-of-work pirate DJs: among the new BBC presenters who had worked on various commercial stations were Mike Ahern, David Allen, Barry Aldis, Tony Blackburn, Pete Brady, Tony Brandon, Dave Cash, Simon Dee, Chris Denning, Pete Drummond, Tom Edwards, Kenny Everett, Keith Fordyce, Allan Freeman, Stuart Henry, Roger Moffat, Pete Murray, John Peel, Emperor Rosko, Ed Stewart, Dave Lee Travis . . .

Radio One burst upon astonished BBC listeners like some kind of strange epidemic. As George Melly pointed out in *The Observer*:

'It was all go at Auntie's first freak-out', he wrote on 1 October. 'The solemnity with which the conventions evolved by the pirate stations have been plagiarised is almost Germanic in its thoroughness: the little bursts of identifying plug music, the compères gabbling over the opening of bars of the records, the fake excitement (*'Beautiful song, beautiful words, must make it!'*) even the deliberate amateurism and fake fear of the sack, are all there. And yet somehow the effect is of a waxwork, absolutely lifelike, but clearly lifeless.'

Radio One has settled down a little since then, though many critical followers of pop still tell you that Radio One has never in fact 'made it' in the sense the pirate stations did; and certainly it seems to be true that the more advanced aspects of pop are badly catered for—except for Derek Jewells' excellent Sunday-night *Sounds Interesting* (characteristically broadcast on Radio Three!).

Of one thing there is, however, no doubt: Radio One has made —or consolidated—a new set of radio stars, some old, some young. Jack Jackson, for instance, was no longer a young man when Radio One opened. He had led a band at the Dorchester before the war, and in the 1940s was one of the best known (and best) trumpeters in the country. Then there was Jimmy Young, a singer who had made over 300 broadcasts by the time he was twenty-four, and in the 1950s had a popular career as a semi-crooner (his biggest hit was *Too Young*). In 1960 he began compèring *Housewives' Choice* (one of the most popular record-request programmes of all time), and since then has consistently held his audiences' attention with a combination of good humour and the sort of amiable idiocy which will always go down well with a majority of older listeners. Sam Costa is another 'old-timer' who has endeared himself to an even larger audience as a DJ.

Jimmy Young, originally a crooner with a golden disc to his credit, runs a record-and-chat show often with a serious content, despite his flip and lively manner

Of the younger comers, Tony Blackburn, is now the doyen. He started life as a singer, when he was in his early twenties, and became a DJ when he joined Radio Caroline South in 1964. With Radio One his career really took off and, though like Jimmy Young he is cordially disliked in some quarters, with his friendliness, his awful jokes, and his enormous talent for identifying with his listeners, he is one of the most successful broadcasters of the 1970s.

Simon Dee's success as a radio DJ led to a brief but meteoric career in television; mainly as a result of over-promotion by the BBC, he crashed from sight. John Dunn joined the Corporation in 1956 as a studio manager; by the 1970s he had established himself as one of the best broadcasters in the business (as several awards testify). Again, his humour helped; though sometimes it led to rather hair-raising moments, as when he told me one of his funniest, mildly filthy stories about half a minute before I was due to start reading a rather solemn news bulletin.

The first few months of Capitol Radio and LBC (a station mainly concerned with news, but actually including every kind of 'chat' from author-interviews to interminable talk-ins and 'phone-ins) were dreadful beyond recall. By 1976 they had

both settled down and, together with the regional commercial stations and the BBC's local broadcasting stations, were providing an acceptable, though less than marvellous, service to a lot of listeners. It is too early to attempt to evaluate them: they have so far only produced one 'star', in George Gale, a journalist who for some time introduced a 'phone-in programme for LBC, and with a gruff air of involvement and impatience built himself a considerable following before his replacement by a more anonymous broadcaster early in 1976.

Even in the context of the switchback-ride of history, it is astonishing how swiftly radio became the most popular medium of communication in the country, and how swiftly it fell away to its present state. Talk to the people in the street, and one finds that very few of them are really aware of radio. Call on someone for an interview, and they start automatically looking for the camera. 'Oh, it's only *radio*', they say, their faces falling.

Certainly there is an extremely keen interest from a minority: there are people who listen critically and enthusiastically to the radio, and who sift the good from the bad, and rejoice or complain accordingly. Radio is still a speedy and spirited medium of communication of news and comment, though there are many

Sharing the kind of compulsive 'niceness', also the trademark of Cliff Richard, Tony Blackburn is probably the best-known of the younger generation of disc-jockeys

criticisms to be made of news broadcasts (and they are made by that growing minority of listeners who, though they live in England, prefer to listen to the news as broadcast on the excellent BBC World Service).

The regular presentation of classical music on Radio Three, though its service has been sadly eroded recently, is envied by many other countries. There is still a considerable concern for drama on Radios Three and Four: full-length productions of the classics are still not uncommon, and there is important new work, together with a great deal of entertaining middle-of-the-road drama of considerable entertainment value.

There are from time to time, as I have said, fine features; the arts are dealt with by *Kaleidoscope*. But there are giant gaps— no regular book programme, for instance; no venture (even, on a regular basis, from *Woman's Hour*—in so many ways that last bastian of good, sound magazine-style radio) into the world of fashion. . . .

And there is still some public concern that the high standards of radio's past should be maintained. The unions connected with broadcasting, together with other organisations such as the Radiowriters' Association of the Society of Authors, and the Writers' Guild, keep a watchful eye, and recently yet another Government committee has been considering broadcasting and its future.

The Pilkington Committee, which produced its Report on broadcasting in 1960, paid relatively little attention to radio. 'We are confident', said the Report, 'that the standard of performance will be sustained.' That confidence has certainly not been betrayed; but it has been perhaps a little strained.

Radio remains an exciting medium. Perhaps, with the development of television, it will now always be a minority medium, and it may be that it must always be a relatively impoverished one. But the development of VHF and the transistor, and the almost universal use of the car radio, means that at peak hours there is probably a larger potential radio audience than ever.

If radio had the money to lure back writers now working in television—writers who would find radio, the natural medium of speech, infinitely more adventurous; if it can cultivate producers who (as is true of a considerable number of men and women now working in the medium) are ready to continue to push back the boundaries; and above all if it is led by men and women of real vision, who do not regard radio as a poor second to television, it could once more command the attention, as it commands the affection, of the nation.

Acknowledgements

There are two major sources of information about the history
of the BBC: the series of 'Handbooks' and 'Yearbooks' which
the Corporation itself has published for over half a century,
and which contain endlessly fascinating material. The second
indispensible source is the *History of Broadcasting in the
United Kingdom*, by Asa Briggs (published by Oxford
University Press; so far three volumes are available—*The
Birth of Broadcasting, The Golden Age of Wireless* and *The
War of Words*). Any reader for whom this present book is an
appetiser, can do no better than to go to Professor Briggs'
highly readable account.

There is a long list of memoirs by professional broadcasters
and ex-members of the BBC. I am particularly grateful to
Messrs Macdonald and Evans for allowing me to reproduce
two passages from *This—is London*, by Stuart Hibberd, and
to Spike Milligan for giving me permission to quote dialogue
from a *Goon Show*.

Unless otherwise credited, the photographs in this book are
reproduced with the kind permission of Radio Times Hulton
Picture Library.

Index

Entries printed in italics are the titles of programmes or series. Figures printed in italic type indicate illustrations but may also refer to textual references on the same page.

159